Wit
The Last Laugh

Des MacHale

PRION

This paperback edition first published in 2000
First published in Great Britain 1999 by
Prion Books Limited,
Imperial Works, Perren Street
London NW5 3ED
www.prionbooks.com

Reprinted 2000

A catalogue record of this book can be obtained
from the British Library

ISBN 1-85375-408-0

Printed and bound in Great Britain by
Creative Print and Design Wales, Ebbw Vale

Wit

The Last Laugh

This book is dedicated to my dear friend and geological companion Charles J. Harold on the occasion of his 80th birthday.

Ad multos annos

Contents

Introduction

Little did I think that when many years ago I first began to jot down on the backs of envelopes every witty quote I came across that I would now be editing my fourth volume of WIT. With the previous *Wit*, followed by the imaginatively titled *More Wit* and the equally imaginatively titled *Yet More Wit*, *Wit – the Last Laugh* surely constitutes the greatest ever collection of witty quotes numbering nearly 8,000 entries.

And the well is not yet dry. As any good fisherman will tell you, there are better fish in the sea than have ever been caught, and I am constantly amazed by the stream of new wit that I encounter every day in newspapers, books, magazines and on video, radio and television.

I am very gratified by the many letters, e-mails and telephone calls I have received from the many readers of WIT worldwide asking me to add their particular favourites to the next collection and of course pointing out the odd misattribution or repetition, for which I apologise profusely. However, since all my quotes are meant to be free standing, sometimes I am forced to take slight liberties with word order, if only to avoid parentheses [which I hate] and for clarity and inclusion of context. For this I make no apology.

So, you lucky reader, you are about to embark on your fourth volume of WIT. ENJOY IT!

Des MacHale
Cork

Art

Art

It might be an idea if Miss Winterson got out her brushes and set to painting her masterpiece as soon as possible. Because the signs are, right now, that she certainly isn't ever going to write one.

Julie Burchill

It is only an auctioneer who can admire all schools of art equally.

Oscar Wilde

One reassuring thing about modern art is that things can't be as bad as they are painted.

Walthall Jackson

Over in the corner the mood was more ruffled, where dense mobs praised 'The 17th Wedding Anniversary: Our Bedroom at Mole End', a seven-sided *tour de force* by Anthony Green RA. It's the kind of picture that induces people to describe it to their companions beside them as if they were blind.

Alex Hamilton

Excuse me guard, where is the big Mona Lisa?

Dave Barry

I've been doing a lot of abstract painting lately, extremely abstract. No brush, no paint, no canvas, I just think about it.

Steven Wright

If my husband Picasso ever met a woman in the street who looked like one of his paintings he would faint.

Jacqueline Roque

To the accountants, a true work of art is an investment that hangs on the wall.

Hilary Alexander

Sculpture is what you bump into when you back up to look at a painting.

Ed Reinhart

Art is making something out of nothing and selling it.

Frank Zappa

Varnishing is the only artistic process with which the Royal Academicians are thoroughly familiar.

Oscar Wilde

At the Art Exhibition fruit sold well, and chickens, and items like corks and shoes, though nudes were slow.

Alex Hamilton

The workmanship was fairly neat and resembled in many ways the kind of barely ingenious handicraft pursued in hospitals by the disabled, who are anxious to employ their fingers without taxing their intellect or senses.

Evelyn Waugh

Art

They couldn't find the artist so they hung the picture.

Frank Zappa

Last year I went fishing with Salvador Dali. He was using a dotted line. He caught every other fish.

Steven Wright

Architecture is the art of how to waste space.

Philip Johnson

Art is anything done by a man or woman on paper, canvas or a musical keyboard that people pretend to understand and sometimes buy.

Elbert Hubbard

I sometimes feel as if I have nothing to say and I want to communicate this.

Damien Hirst

A ship ran aground carrying a cargo of red and black paints. The whole crew was marooned.

William Bishop

I just keep painting until I feel like pinching the flesh tones of the nudes. Then I know it's night.

Pierre Auguste Renoir

He was probably our greatest living painter – until he died.

Will Rogers

Rembrandt is not to be compared in the painting of character with our extraordinarily gifted English artist, Mr Rippingille.

John Hunt

There is a thin line between genius and insanity. I have erased that line.

Oscar Levant

I couldn't have a modern painting hanging in my home. It would be like living with a gas leak.

Edith Evans

There is something wrong with a work of art if it can be understood by a policeman.

Patrick Kavanagh

If you want to be an artist, declare your intention to create a composition and start a piece at some time. Then cause something to happen over a period of time and end the piece at some time, or keep it going telling everyone it is 'work in progress'. Finally, get a part-time job so you can continue to do stuff like this.

Frank Zappa

I believe that a real composer writes for no other purpose than to please himself. Those who compose because they want to please others and have audiences in mind are not artists.

Arnold Schoenberg

The stars are not bad, but there are decidedly too many of them, and they are not very well arranged. I would have done it differently.

James McNeill Whistler

The Arts Council doesn't believe in supporting amateurs, except in its own ranks.

John Drummond

We must remember that art is art. Still, on the other hand, water is water – and east is east and west is west, and if you take cranberries and stew them like apple sauce, they taste much more like prunes than rhubarb does.

Groucho Marx

'Woman with Hat' was a tremendous effort on the part of Matisse, a thing brilliant and powerful, but the nastiest smear of paint I had ever seen.

Leo Stein

I will be so brief I have already finished.

Salvador Dali

Business and Money

Business and Money

The difference between a man and his valet is that they both smoke the same cigars but only one pays for them.

Robert Frost

To stop telephone salesmen in their tracks I always say 'That's great. I'm very interested but I'm busy right now, so if you could leave your home number I'll call you back tonight at about 11:30pm'.

Bob Jeffay

Banking is the second oldest profession but more profitable than the oldest profession.

Flann O'Brien

An Act of God designation on all insurance policies means roughly that you cannot be insured for the accidents that are most likely to happen to you.

Alan Coren

Noah must have taken into the Ark two taxes, one male and one female and did they multiply beautifully! Next to guinea pigs, taxes must have been the most prolific animals.

Will Rogers

George goes to sleep at a bank every day from ten to four, except Saturdays, when they wake him up and put him outside at two.

Jerome K. Jerome

Things got so bad that I received a letter from The Readers' Digest, saying that I hadn't been included in their prize draw.
John McGrath

Everybody likes a kidder, but nobody will lend him money.

Arthur Miller

An economist is someone who, if you have forgotten your telephone number, will estimate it for you.

Edward Kent

One of the silliest wastes of time is figuring out how much money you'd have if you'd stayed single.

Kin Hubbard

Doubtless there are things money won't buy, but I cannot think of any of them at the moment.
Richard Needham

Time spent in the advertising business seems to create a permanent deformity like the Chinese habit of foot-binding.
Dean Acheson

I'd give a thousand dollars to be a millionaire.
Lewis Timberlake

If you had your life to live over again – you'd need a lot more money.

Robert Orben

I would like to execute everyone who uses the word 'fair' in connection with income tax policies.

William F. Buckley

Nothing in the known universe travels faster than a bad cheque.

Alec Slick

God made gentiles because somebody has to buy retail.

Arthur Naiman

There is a certain Buddhistic calm that comes from having money in the bank.

Tom Robbins

There's no business like show business, but there are several businesses like accounting.

David Letterman

Oil prices have fallen lately. We include this news for the benefit of gas stations, which otherwise wouldn't learn of it for six months.

Bill Tammeus

Business and Money

We will spare no expense to save money on this movie.

Samuel Goldwyn

It is a rather pleasant experience to be alone in a bank at night.

Willie Sutton

I have long admired the unknown genius, larcenous though he must have been, who ran this one-line ad in a Los Angeles newspaper: LAST DAY TO SEND IN YOUR DOLLAR BOX 153. Thousands of idiots sent in their dollars.

Leo Rosten

Breathes there a man with a soul so dead that he doesn't stick two fingers in the coin return box after completing a call.

Richard Needham

I got this letter telling me I may already be a loser.

Rodney Dangerfield

There is a very easy way to return from a casino with a small fortune – go there with a large one.

Jack Yelton

The only difference between a tax collector and a taxidermist is that a taxidermist leaves the hide.

Mortimer Caplan

One of the greatest wits of all time was the person who called them easy payments.

George Burns

High finance isn't burglary or obtaining money by false pretences, but rather a judicious selection from the best features of those fine arts.

Finley Peter Dunne

I once worked as a salesman and was very independent. I took orders from no one.

Jacques Barzun

I think 'immoral' is probably the wrong word to use in relation to insider trading. I prefer the word 'unethical.'

Ivan Boesky

If you can count your money you're not rich.

J. Paul Getty

Honesty pays, but it doesn't seem to pay enough to suit some people.

Kin Hubbard

I like thieves. Some of my best friends are thieves. Why just last week we had the president of the bank for dinner.

W.C. Fields

If anyone ever came to Sheridan asking him to repay a loan, instead of giving them money, he actually borrowed more.

William Hazlitt

'King-sized' seems to be modelled on Edward the Eight, who stood 5ft 2ins in his socks.

Russell Ash

Oxford does not need any new buildings, nor does it need a business school, which is bound to attract undesirables.

Auberon Waugh

This is far and away the finest depression we have ever had.

Henry Ford

Not every problem someone has with his girlfriend is necessarily due to the capitalist mode of production.

Herbert Marcuse

I cannot say whether the tonnage of the beef quota from Australia to Japan will be the same, more than, or less than the previous one. But it will definitely fall into one of these three options.

Yoshio Okawara

Americans travelling abroad are so disorientated by foreign currency that every now and then one of them will buy a single croissant and leave a tip large enough for the waiter to retire for life.

Dave Barry

Meetings are indespensable when you don't want to do anything.

J.K. Galbraith

What is a crook but a businessman without an office?

Brendan Behan

Money can't buy happiness. It can however rent it.

Gregory Singleton

Cash slips from my hands into the bookies' hands as if it were magnetised.

Phil Silvers

I was walking down the street and there was a sign stapled to a telephone pole. It said 'Lost $50. Reward: If found just keep it'.

Steven Wright

We don't have American Express in Russia. However, we do have Russian Express. It's slogan is 'Don't Leave Home'.

Yakov Smirnoff

How happy I should be if only I could get five hundred pounds deeper in debt than I am already.

Henry Fielding

You can't help liking my boss because if you don't he fires you.

Joey Adams

A fool and his money are soon married.

Carolyn Wells

My typing is really speeding up – I now can make twenty mistakes per minute.

Goldie Hawn

Remember in the time it takes to read this, Bill Gates has made another million dollars.

Patrick Murray

A fool and his money are soon parted – who got yours?

Henny Youngman

The financial cost of playing golf can best be figured out when you realise if you were to devote the same time and energy to business you would be a millionaire in approximately six weeks.

Buddy Hackett

Every crowd has a silver lining.

Phineas T. Barnum

Nothing increases the value of a cow and so quickly as to get killed by a train.

Donald Gordon

I am a gentleman – I live by robbing the poor.

George Bernard Shaw

People will buy anything that is one to a customer.

Sinclair Lewis

I would have made a first class tramp, if I'd had more money.

Robert Morley

My wife went into a bank and asked if she could open a joint account. When the clerk asked her with whom, she replied, 'Someone with lots of money of course'.

Don Foreman

You look like someone who owes me money.

Tony Ianuzzi

People want economy and they will pay any price to get it.

Lee Iacocca

If you can't find it in the index, look very carefully through the entire catalogue.

Sears Roebuck

If I found the end of the rainbow, Murphy would be there to tell me the pot of gold is at the other end.

Bert Whitney

Fifteen cents of every twenty-cent stamp goes on storage.

Louis Rukeyser

A person who can't pay, gets another person who can't pay, to guarantee that he can pay.

Charles Dickens

Once you're safely in the mall, you should tie your children to you with ropes so the other Christmas shoppers won't try to buy them. Holiday shoppers have been whipped into a frenzy by months of holiday advertisements, and they will buy anything small enough to stuff into a shopping bag.

Dave Barry

Honest businessmen should be protected from the unscrupulous consumer.

Lester Maddox

We are going to continue having these meetings, every day, until I find out why no work is getting done.

Gary Larson

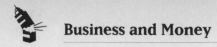

Inside the jars were discovered six parchment scrolls with ancient incomprehensible writing which the shepherd, in his ignorance, sold to the museum for $750,000 apiece.

Woody Allen

An economist is a man who states the obvious in terms of the incomprehensible.

Alfred Knopf

Sophisticated econometric models have successfully predicted fourteen of the last three recessions.

Alfred Conway

$100 invested at seven percent interest for a hundred years will become $100,000, at which time it will be worth absolutely nothing.

Lazarus Long

Fame is failure disguised as money.

Brendan Behan

After a long trek in the cold to get there, the monks would offer to sell you a cup of coffee. You had a choice: there was the two-dollar cup or a two hundred dollar cup. When pressed to explain the difference, the monks would say, 'A hundred and ninety-eight dollars'.

Steve Perry

Business and Money

For several days before you put it in the mail, carry your tax return around under your armpit. No IRS agent is going to want to spend hours poring over a sweat-stained document.

Dave Barry

Bank failures are caused by depositors who don't deposit enough money to cover losses due to mismanagement.

Dan Quayle

True, money can't buy you happiness, but it isn't happiness I want, it's money.

Frank Bizarro

My father worked in a bank and they caught him stealing pens.

Rodney Dangerfield

There is no such thing as an innocent purchaser of stocks.

Louis Brandeis

Keep Paddy behind the big mixer.

Alfred McAlpine

My friends, money is not all. It is not money that will mend a broken heart or reassemble the fragments of a dream. Money cannot brighten the hearth nor repair the portals of a shattered home. I refer of course to Confederate money.

Artemus Ward

Drink and other Drugs

Drink and other Drugs

In the pub last night I had six beers, two large gins, a couple of Ports, a brandy and a pork pie. On the way home I was as sick as a dog. I don't think that pork pie agreed with me.
Rex Jameson

There was an ancient Greek law which made it a crime not to get drunk during the annual festival of Dionysus.
Bruce Felton

The heavy port drinker must be prepared to make some sacrifice of personal beauty and agility.
Evelyn Waugh

I like the odd drink. Five is odd, seven is odd, nine is odd…
W.C. Fields

The only thing worse than a reformed cigarette smoker is an early Christmas shopper.
Liz Scott

I once ate a cannabis cookie but I didn't swallow.
Sandy Toksvig

I find that red wine improves with age. The older I get the more I like it.
Raymond George

The best temperance lecture I ever heard was delivered by a man under the influence of alcohol.
W.C. Fields

Drink and other Drugs

In 1969 I gave up drinking and sex. It was the worst twenty minutes of my life.

George Best

No, I don't mind if you smoke – not if you don't mind my being sick all over you.

Thomas Beecham

I am so holy that when I touch wine it turns into water.

Aga Khan III

I was with some Vietnamese recently, and some of them were smoking two cigarettes at the same time. That's the kind of customers we need.

Jesse Helms

All roads lead to rum.

W.C. Fields

He was a wine waiter at a great hotel, endowed by nature with a uniquely sensitive nose and a retentive memory. No drop had ever passed his lips, but when it came to the test he was able to name the chateau and year of a dozen clarets merely by putting his nose to the glass. He was like a sanitary inspector smelling drains.

Evelyn Waugh

I myself once woke up in a drawer at the bottom of a wardrobe. That was fairly frightening. Try opening a drawer from the inside. It's quite tricky.

Jeffrey Bernard

Drink and other Drugs

How do you look when I'm sober?

Ring Lardner

When my time comes, I want to die in bed, listening to music and sampling a warming well-rounded twenty-five-year-old. I mean whisky of course.

Tom Brown

When Jack Benny throws a party, you not only bring your own scotch, you bring your own rocks.

George Burns

Whisky-making is the art of making poison pleasant.

Samuel Johnson

The European Parliment has banned smoking by its MPs while it is in session. The reason is that those fellows drink so much that if you lit a match in there the place would explode.

Eamon Morrissey

A soft drink turneth away company.

Oliver Herford

On one occasion some one put a very little wine into a wine-cooler and said that it was sixteen years old. 'It's very small for its age', remarked his guest.

Athenaeus

Red sky in the morning – red wine the previous evening.

Don Rickles

He'd had so much the night before he was suddenly sick over the bride. The service continued a while and then the groom was sick again, this time over the vicar.

Jeffrey Bernard

A good general rule on wine-tasting is to state that the bouquet is better than the taste, and vice versa.

Stephen Potter

Twenty four hours in a day; twenty four beers in a case – mere coincidence?

Steven Wright

Don't invite drug addicts round for a meal on Boxing Day. They may find your offer of 'cold turkey' embarrassing or offensive.

Steven Howlett

I've been doing the Fonda workout: the Peter Fonda workout. That's where I wake up, take a hit of acid, smoke a joint, and go to my sister's house and ask her for money.

Kevin Meaney

People may say what they like about the decay of Christianity; the religious system that produced green Chartreuse can never really die.

H.H. Munro

Drink and other Drugs

The whiskey went down my throat like a torchlight procession.

John L. O'Sullivan

I certainly do not drink all the time. I have to sleep you know.

W.C. Fields

Cannabis Television, an Amsterdam-based TV venture to promote 'the positive side' of marijuana use, appears to have gone up in smoke. Just a few hours before the broadcast deadline for the one-hour pilot programme, the channel's staff abandoned the project, apparently too stoned to carry on.

Mark Fuller

I love to smoke and I love to eat red meat and I only eat red meat that comes from cows that smoke. They're special cows that grow in Virginia with voice boxes in their necks.

Denis Leary

The two-headed boy in the circus never had such a headache as I have.

W.C. Fields

Christmas is the alcoholidays.

Sigmund Freud

If you drink raicilla straight down, you can feel it going into each individual intestine.

Richard Burton

Drink and other Drugs

I once accidentally dropped a bottle of whisky overboard from a plane and without hesitation dived after it.

W.C. Fields

I met a manager of a funeral home. He gave me a card which said 'Thank you for smoking'.

John Dillon

A cigarette is the perfect type of a perfect pleasure. It is exquisite, and it leaves one unsatisfied. What more can one want?

Oscar Wilde

There are two kinds of people in the world – normal human beings with an aversion to telling outright lies while staring directly into people's faces, and tobacco lobbyists.

Will Durst

I used to be a bartender at the Betty Ford Clinic.

Steven Wright

I have made an important discovery, that alcohol, taken in sufficient quantity, produces all the effects of intoxication.

Oscar Wilde

Lord, grant me the serenity to accept the things I cannot change, the courage to change the things I can, and the wisdom to hide the bodies of those I had to kill because they pissed me off.

Emo Philips

Drink and other Drugs

I don't do drugs anymore because I find I get the same effect just by standing up really fast.

Jonathan Katz

There are two things a highlander likes naked and one of them is whisky.

Fulton McKay

I asked an alcoholic doctor how he first knew he was an alcoholic and he told me it was when he sprayed vaginal deodorant on a man's face.

Jeffrey Bernard

The British Empire was created by men who never drew a sober breath after the age of seven.

John Doxat

Fortune knocks at every man's door once in life, but in a good many cases the man is in a neighbouring saloon and does not hear her.

Mark Twain

Education

In the event of a nuclear attack Scottish children will be given a day off school.

Vin Shanley

There are only two sorts of job always open under the English social system – domestic service and education. However abominable one's record, though one may be fresh from prison or the lunatic asylum, one can always look after the silver or teach the young. I had not the right presence for a footman, so I chose the latter.

Evelyn Waugh

A man who has never gone to school may steal from a freight car, but if he has a university education, he may steal the whole railroad.

Franklin D. Roosevelt

Teaching has ruined more American novelists than drink.

Gore Vidal

And remember, this is the school play. You are not here to enjoy yourselves.

Alan Bennett

I swear I once saw this notice in a shop window –
     AVAILABLE TOP CLASS TYPISSED.

Patrick Murray

All of my best thoughts were stolen by the ancients.

Ralph Waldo Emerson

Seventy eight percent of our high school students in a recent nationwide multiple choice test, identified Abraham Lincoln as 'a kind of lobster'. That's right: more than three quarters of our nation's youth could not correctly identify the man who invented the telephone.

Dave Barry

H.G. Wells' *History of the World* is very good until the end of the Neolithic.

A. J. P. Taylor

I had an IQ test but the results came back negative.

Steven Wright

The fellow who thinks he knows it all is especially annoying to those of us who do.

Harold Coffin

If a word in the dictionary is misspelled, how would we know?

Steven Wright

I am returning this otherwise good typing paper to you because somebody has printed gibberish all over it and put your name at the top.

Steven Clark

I have never been jealous. Not even when my dad finished fifth grade a year before I did.

Jeff Foxworthy

Education

You live and learn. Well at any rate you live.

Douglas Adams

A gifted teacher is as rare as a gifted doctor and makes far less money.

Tom Lehrer

Don Robustiano had never read Voltaire, but he detested him as much as Gloucester, the Archdeacon, detested him, who hadn't read him either.

Leopoldo Alas

My teacher must have known me, had he seen me as he was wont to see me, for he was in the habit of flogging me constantly. Perhaps he did not recognise me by my face.

Anthony Trollope

When the children at public schools should have been whipped and taught Greek paradigms, they were set arguing about birth control and nationalisation. Their crude little opinions were treated with respect. It is hardly surprising that they were Bolshevik at 18 and bored at 20.

Evelyn Waugh

Force is all that matters. War is sacred. Hanging is excellent. We don't need too much knowledge. Build more prisons and fewer schools.

Victor Hugo

A University President is like the body at an Irish wake. They need you in order to have the party, but no one expects you to say very much.

Anthony Lake

I think the world is run by 'C' students.

Al McGuire

What are we going to do about ignorance and apathy? I don't know and I don't care.

William Safire

Children's alphabet blocks should contain a warning: Letters may be used to construct phrases and sentences that may be deemed offensive.

David Handelsman

If you had to have a diploma to collect unemployment benefit, you'd see a lot more kids staying in school.

Wayne Knight

The private schools of England are to the educated classes what the Union Workhouses are to the very poor. Relief is granted to all who come but it is provided in as unpalatable a form as possible.

Evelyn Waugh

The need to use the lavatory is not related to biological urges but an urge to get out of class.

William Marsano

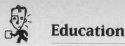

Education

The survey showed that, in a class of 21, not one pupil knew what marmalade was, and a sixth-class pupil who saw horses being fed with nose bags, on a school tour, thought they were sniffing glue.

John Golds

The splendid thing about education is that everyone wants it and, like influenza, you can give it away without losing any of it yourself.

Evelyn Waugh

My retirement from teaching was a most blessed event. Five years, and I still thrive on the absence of students.

Henry Holmes Smith

To give an accurate description of what never happened is the proper occupation of the historian.

Oscar Wilde

Nor can I do better, in conclusion, than impress upon you the study of Greek literature, which not only elevates above the vulgar herd, but leads not infrequently to positions of considerable emolument.

Thomas Gaisford

Genius may have its limitations but stupidity is not thus handicapped.

Elbert Hubbard

What's on your mind, if you'll forgive the overstatement?

Fred Allen

A law of academic life is that it is impossible to be excessive in flattery of one's peers.

David Lodge

Eight concerned parents in rural Georgia have sued the local school district for teaching their children the alphabet which can be used to form dirty words.

Dave Barry

Introducing 'lite' the new way to spell 'light' but with twenty percent fewer letters.

Jerry Seinfeld

The philosophy exam was a piece of cake – which was a bit of a surprise because I was expecting some questions on a piece of paper.

Emo Philips

Without remarking that the thing became a trumpet in his hands, say something relevant about Milton's sonnets.

Stephen Potter

When there are two Ph.Ds from a developing country, one is Head of State and the other is in exile.

Lord Samuel

Education

Seamus Kavanagh attempted to write a comprehensive dictionary of the Irish language but was stranded on a psychological plateau on the letter H for many years.

Alfred O'Rahilly

One never knows, do one?

Fats Waller

My father must have had some elementary education for he could read and write and keep accounts inaccurately.

George Bernard Shaw

Life is a test, only a test. If this was a real life, you would have been instructed where to go and what to do.

Jeff Hammond

Lack of education is an extraordinary handicap when one is being offensive.

Josephine Tey

Ask five economists a question and you'll get five different answers (six if one went to Harvard).

Edgar Fiedler

He pursued his studies but never overtook them.

H. G. Wells

What the heck is an FAQ?

John Hunter

I am what is called a professor emeritus, from the latin 'e',
out, and meritus, 'so he ought to be'.

Stephen Leacock

First come I; my name is Jowett.
There's no knowledge but I know it.
I am Master of this college:
What I don't know isn't knowledge.

H.C. Beeching

Women at Cambridge were not entitled to BA Cantab; only
to BA (Tit), which understandably few espoused.

Valerie Grove

Subjunctive to the last, he preferred to ask 'And that, sir,
would be the Hippodromeí?'

Alexander Woollcott

Food

Food

No request is too much in this restaurant – I shall of course be delighted to change your colostomy bag Ma'am.

Jonathan Meades

Soup is food – not musical instrument.

Charlie Chan

Diamond Jim Brady was the best twenty-five customers I ever had in my restaurant.

Charles Rector

My uncle Charlie showed me where milk comes from, but I still like it.

Hank Ketcham

I'm trying to lose some weight so I've gone on a garlic diet. You eat garlic with everything. It doesn't make you lose any weight but people stand further back and you look thinner at a distance.

Noel Britton

Bread that must be sliced with an axe is bread that is too nourishing.

Fran Lebowitz

The two biggest sellers in any bookshop are the cookbooks and the diet books. The cookbooks tell you how to prepare the food and the diet books tell you how not to eat any of it.

Andy Rooney

At my lemonade stand I used to give the first glass away free and charge five dollars for the second glass. The refill contained the antidote.

Emo Philips

The proof that God has a very weird sense of humour is that, having invented the sublime mystery of haute cuisine, he went and give it to the French.

A.A. Gill

One of the main arguments in favour of fox hunting is that foxes kill chickens. But so does Bernard Matthews and nobody advocates chasing him across the country with a pack of dogs and tearing him to pieces.

Alexei Sayle

Shake and shake the ketchup bottle. First none'll come and then a lott'ill.

Richard Armour

There is a machine that dispenses liquids that are allegedly 'coffee', 'tea', 'hot chocolate' and even 'soup', which all come from the same orifice and all taste exactly the same.

Dave Barry

Another machine dispenses bags containing a grand total of maybe three potato chips each and packages of crackers smeared with a bizarre substance called 'cheez', which is the same bright-orange colour as marine rescue equipment.

Dave Barry

Food

Remember a dog is not only for Christmas – there should be plenty left for Boxing Day and the day after.

Freddie Starr

Avoid fruits and nuts. You are what you eat.

Jim Davis

Dog biscuits help freshen your breath and prevent tartar.

Mel Gibson

This recipe is certainly silly. It says to separate two eggs, but it doesn't say how far to separate them.

Gracie Allen

A man cannot have a pure mind who refuses apple-dumplings.

Samuel Taylor Coleridge

Willpower is being able to eat just one salted peanut.

Pat Elphinstone

In a corner of the kitchen they found a dozen bottles bearing the labels of various mineral waters – Evian, St. Galmiet, Vichy, Malvern – all empty. It was Mr Youkoumian's practice to replenish them, when required, from the foetid well at the back of the house.

Evelyn Waugh

It is not true that I never eat vegetables.   I once ate a pea.

Beau Brummell

Coffee in a fast food restaurant should be allowed to cool before being applied to the groin area.

Elden Carnahan

In luncheon parties in old days, the remains of the guests were taken away with the debris of the feast.

Oscar Wilde

Thou canst not serve both cod and salmon.

Ada Leverson

Never dine in a restaurant where the speciality of the house is the Heimlich manoeuvre.

Victor Lewis-Smith

I have my own chopsticks. They have my initials on the top. And Velcro on the bottom.

Rita Rudner

Nothing takes the taste out of peanut butter quite like unrequited love.

Charlie Brown

Some day George Bernard Shaw will eat a pork chop and then God help all women.

Beatrice Tanner

Food

Brown sauce is the most extraordinary concoction. Only a nation that thought of food as an extension of engineering could have invented brown sauce. You can clean silver with it. It doesn't go with anything. It's a culinary assassin, an olfactory blackout. And it's got tamarinds in it: ''Ere guv, we've got these weird little fruit from out east. What will we do with them?' 'Chuck 'em in the brown sauce'.

A.A. Gill

The French cook – the English open tins.

John Galsworthy

My favourite sexual fantasy is smearing my naked body with chocolate and cream and being left in a room on my own to eat it.

Jo Brand

I was a vegetarian until I started leaning toward the sunlight.

Rita Rudner

You can tell a lot about a fellow's character by his way of eating jellybeans.

Ronald Reagan

He was a legend in his own lunchtime.

Christopher Wordsworth

I once bought a cellphone that had a little sticker on the box that said DO NOT EAT PACKAGING MATERIAL. There went another freebie snack at the office.

Andreas Skau

Ask not what you can do for your country, ask what's for lunch.

Orson Welles

I would be going against my religion if I drank tea or coffee.

Brendan Behan

We have a Russian nursery rhyme that goes "Old Mother Hubbard went to the cupboard to get her poor dog". That sounds pretty gross until you see an American eating a hot dog. In Russia we don't eat that part of the dog.

Yakov Smirnoff

In Mexico we have a word for sushi: bait.

Jose Simon

When I was a nurse my favourite assignment was the anorexic ward. I sometimes ate as many as seventeen dinners.

Jo Brand

To eat is to perform successively and successfully the functions of mastication, humectation, and deglutition.

Ambrose Bierce

Food

One tribe invited me to dinner, an excellent repast
beginning with whale.

W.C. Fields

Statistics show that of those who contract the habit of eating,
very few will survive.

William Irwin

Romanian-Yiddish cooking has killed more Jews than
Hitler.

Zero Mostel

A recipe for the festive season – turkey with popcorn
dressing. Stuff the turkey and bake at 325° for about five
hours, or until the popcorn blows the turkey's ass clean
across the room.

Reinhold Aman

It's all right Arthur – the white wine came up with the fish.

Herman J. Mankiewicz

There's a new diet. You eat whatever you want whenever
you want, and as much as you want. You don't lose any
weight, but it's really easy to stick to.

George Tucker

The easiest way to make a fruit cake is to buy a darkish cake,
then pound some old, hard fruit into it with a mallet. Be
sure to wear safety glasses.

Dave Barry

I was out at one restaurant and they didn't have prices on the menu. Just faces with different expressions of horror.

Rita Rudner

By the time they had diminished from fifty to eight, the other dwarves began to suspect 'Hungry'.

Gary Larson

'What will you have?' said the waiter, reflectively picking his nose. 'I'll have two boiled eggs, you bastard, you can't get your fingers in those'.

George Wallace

My wife, inviting me to sample her very first soufflé, accidently dropped a spoonful of it on my foot, fracturing several small bones.

Woody Allen

The man is a common murderer, possibly, but a very uncommon cook.

H.H. Munro

When the waitress puts the dinner on the table, the old men look at the dinner. The young men look at the waitress.

Gelett Burgess

Mustard is no good without roast beef.

Chico Marx

Food

I saw him even now going the way of all flesh, that is to say towards the kitchen.

John Webster

A quarter ounce of chocolate equals four pounds of fat.

Joan Rivers

A menu is a list of dishes that a restaurant has just run out of.

Erma Bombeck

Last week I went to a store to look for a decaffeinated coffee table. They couldn't help me.

Steven Wright

'Au contraire', as the man said when asked if he'd dined on the boat.

G.K. Chesterton

I miss my wife's cooking – as often as I can.

Henny Youngman

Red meat is not bad for you. Now blue-green meat, that's bad for you.

Tommy Smothers

I'll give you an idea how bad my cooking is – last Christmas the family bought me an oven that flushes.

Phyllis Diller

Lawyers and other Professions

This book is dedicated to Gollancz's libel lawyer, John Rubinstein, without whom it would have been considerably longer.

Victor Lewis-Smith

Your honour, as I was overtaking the other car quite legally, the policeman was hiding in the bushes with a bucket of whitewash, and when he saw me approach he rushed out and painted double lines on the road.

Spike Milligan

I was going to be a shrink but I thought if their stories got dull, I'd have to kill them.

Ruby Wax

We had a guy who was absent from work so much that he celebrated his 25th anniversary with the company after 35 years.

Gene Perret

Of this I am certain, when the Antichrist comes, he will have a law degree.

John F. Curran

Pool hustling is life – work is for cowards.

U.J. Puckett

The witness will please state her age, after which the clerk will swear her in.

Norton Plasset

We have a criminal jury system which is superior to any in the world; and its efficiency is marred only by the difficulty of finding twelve men every day who don't know anything and can't read.

Mark Twain

Lawyers and other Professions

If I was being executed by injection, I'd clean up my cell real neat. Then, when they came to get me I'd say, 'Injection?' I thought you said 'inspection'. They'd probably feel real bad, and maybe I could get out of it.

Jack Handey

The comparative of lawyer is "liar" and the superlative is "expert".

Pierre Bernthsen

When Lem Moon was acquitted for the murder of his wife and the judge asked him if he had anything to say he replied, 'If I had known I'd have to go through so much red tape, I never would have shot her'.

Kin Hubbard

Anyone who supports capital punishment should be shot.

Colin Crompton

The First Amendment states that members of religious groups, no matter how small or unpopular, shall have the right to hassle you in airports.

Dave Barry

Lawyers are the opposite of sex. Even when they're good they're lousy.

Dave Barry

Wretches hang that jurymen may dine.

Alexander Pope

The ugliest of trades have their moments of pleasure. Now if I were a grave-digger, or even a hangman, there are some people I could work for with a great deal of enjoyment.

Douglas Jerrold

Nurses are a styleless regiment of women making the worst of several worlds. They are hygienic but coarse, unsympathetic but fussy.

Quentin Crisp

It is against the law to commit suicide in this town, although what the law can do to a guy who commits suicide I am never able to figure out.

Damon Runyon

Lawyers are the only persons in whom ignorance of the law is not punished.

Jeremy Bentham

There is no satisfaction in hanging a man who does not object to it.

George Bernard Shaw

I believe that many people would be alive today if there were a death penalty.

Nancy Reagan

If it weren't for my lawyer, I'd still be in prison. Two people can dig a lot faster than one.

Mister Boffo

Many lawyers, I suppose, were children once.

Charles Lamb

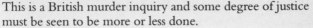

This is a British murder inquiry and some degree of justice must be seen to be more or less done.

Tom Stoppard

English law prohibits a man from marrying his mother-in-law. This is a perfect example of totally unnecessary legislation.

Clement Freud

Mr President, do not let so great an achievement as the US acquisition of the Panama Canal Zone suffer from any taint of legality.

Philander Knox

A Gentleman's Agreement is an arrangement which is not an agreement, between two persons, neither of whom is a gentleman, with each expecting the other to be strictly bound while he himself has no intention of being bound at all.

Justice Vaisey

Tea person required. Ladies of either sex may apply.

Michael Green

Have I any last request? Yes, a bulletproof vest please.

James Rodgers

I've gone into hundreds of fortune-teller's parlours, and have been told thousands of things, but nobody's ever told me I was a policewoman getting ready to arrest her.

Jane Pitman

The closest a person ever comes to perfection is when he fills out a job application form.

Stanley Randall

Being an MP is the sort of job all working class parents want for their children – clean, indoors and no heavy lifting.

Diane Abbott

I once stuck my head out of the window and got arrested for mooning.

Rodney Dangerfield

You can help the local police by popping in to the mortuary each day to see if you can identify any of the bodies.

Lewis Maitland

A judge is not supposed to know anything about the facts of life until they have been presented in evidence and explained to him at least three times.

Hubert Parker

He was in the Navy when Long John Silver had two legs and an egg on his shoulder.

Michael Green

Why does Washington have so many one-way streets? So that all the civil servants coming in late won't collide with those going home early.

Arnie Benjamin

Lawyers and other Professions

You can always tell a good explosives expert. He has all of his fingers and does not speak in a high-pitched voice.

Blaster Bates

The lawyer's prayer – Stir up much strife among thy people, O Lord, lest thy servant perish.

Sam Ervin

Make lots of money. Enjoy the work. Operate within the law. Choose any two of three.

Jack Dee

There are seven natural openings in the head and body. A lawyer is the only human being with eight. The extra one is a slot to store the money in, should his bank be unable to hold all of it.

W.C. Fields

You have the right to remain silent – forever.

Clint Eastwood

The Lord Chief Justice of England recently said that the greater part of his judicial time was spent investigating collisions between propelled vehicles, each on its own side of the road, each sounding its horn and each stationary.

Philip Guedella

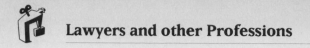

Lawyers and other Professions

By the argument of counsel it was shown that at half past ten in the morning on the day of the murder, the accused became insane and remained so for eleven and a half hours exactly.

Mark Twain

I did not call Hillary Clinton a 'congenital liar'. I was misquoted. I called her a 'congenial lawyer'.

William Safire

Epitaph for a dead waiter – at last God caught his eye.

Harry Secombe

A broad definition of crime in England is any lower-class activity that is displeasing to the upper classes.

Anthony Jay

The British police force used to be run by men of integrity. That is a mistake which has been rectified.

Joe Orton

My child was inmate of the month at our local Juvenile Detention Facility.

Monica Norling

How did I become a chimney-sweep? I took a correspondence course.

Richard Haslam

Lawyers and other Professions

I'm totally against capital punishment myself, except for really serious crimes like plumbers who promise to show up at 9:00 am and don't appear until the following Tuesday when they leave a note saying 'We called to unblock your pipes, but you were out!'

Kenny Everett

My agent went swimming in shark-infested waters but escaped without injury. That's what they call professional courtesy.

Herman J. Mankiewicz

Be so kind, members of the jury, to turn the matter over in what you are pleased to call your minds.

Richard Bethell

I am surprised that so many people turn to crime when there are so many legal ways to be dishonest.

Al Capone

The difference between fantasy and science fiction is that one has honest politicians, scrupulous lawyers and altruistic doctors, while the other has only beings from outer space.

William Watkins

It is one of the tragedies of our time to see women making a nuisance of themselves as welfare officers when they could be employed as nursery maids.

Auberon Waugh

Lawyers and other Professions

They say machinery is going to take the place of every profession in the world but that's something she never need worry about.

Herman J. Mankiewicz

I was provided with additional input that was radically different from the truth and I assisted in furthering that version.

Oliver North

As your attorney it is my duty to inform you that it is not important that you understand what I'm doing or why you are paying me so much money. What is important is that you continue to do so.

Hunter S. Thompson

The Grand Old Duke of York
He had ten thousand men.
His case comes up next week.

Spike Milligan

Literature

Literature

You've got to be one of two ages to appreciate Walter Scott. When you're eighteen you can read *Ivanhoe*, and you want to wait until you are ninety to read some of the rest. It takes a pretty well-regulated abstemious critic to live ninety years.

Mark Twain

I cannot choose one hundred best books because I have written only five.

Oscar Wilde

I wouldn't drop God if I were Graham Greene. It would be like P.G. Wodehouse dropping Jeeves halfway through the Wooster series.

Evelyn Waugh

I trust that the Brownings' marriage will be a happy one and that they will speak more intelligibly to each other than they have yet done to the public.

William Wordsworth

I was once gratified to receive a cheque from a magazine for a joke I had stolen from its own pages.

Bernard Braden

The poetical works of Southey will be read when those of Shakespeare and Milton are forgotten – but not till then.

Richard Porson

And now kind friends, what I have wrote
I hope you will pass over,
and not criticise as some have done
Hitherto herebefore.

Julia A. Moore

I have met people who have borrowed my books from the library; I have met others more enterprising, who have stolen them from the library; but I have never met anyone who has *bought* any of my books.

Russell Braddon

A prose style may often be improved by striking out every other word from each sentence when written.

Sydney Smith

I hear the little children say
(For the tale will never die)
How the old pump flowed both night and day
When the brooks and the wells ran dry.
This verse has all the ring of Macaulay in it, and is a form of poetry which cannot possibly harm anybody, even if translated into French.

Oscar Wilde

On looking over at Sir Walter Scott, I was painfully struck by the utter vacancy of his look. How dreadful if he should live to survive that mighty mind of his.

Thomas Moore

Literature

This book was written in those long hours I spent waiting
for my wife to get dressed to go out. And if she had never
gotten dressed at all, this book would never have been
written.

Groucho Marx

My talent I put into my writing; my genius I have saved for
living.

Oscar Wilde

Writers have two main problems. One is writer's block,
when words won't come at all, and the other is logorrhoea,
when the words come so fast that they can hardly get to the
wastebasket in time.

Cecilia Bartholomew

The football memoir is a literary form that ranks at least two
grades below the trashiest airport novel.

Alan English

Women write novels because there is this tremendous desire
to expose themselves; with men the motive is often some
kind of obscure revenge.

Auberon Waugh

I once came across a book I had signed 'With compliments'
to a friend in a second hand bookshop. So I bought it and
sent it to him 'With renewed compliments'.

George Bernard Shaw

In truth, Wycherley's indecency is protected against the critics as a skunk is protected against the hunters. It is safe because it is too filthy to handle, and too noisome to approach.

Thomas B. Macaulay

Always be nicer to writers younger than you, because they are the ones who will be writing about you.

Cyril Connolly

William Faulkner was a great friend of mine. Well as much as you could be a friend of his unless you were a fourteen-year-old nymphet.

Truman Capote

The few bad poems which occasionally are created during abstinence are of no great interest.

Wilhelm Reich

Henry Miller was writing a huge book on Hamlet but could not bring himself to read Shakespeare's version; so he asked Lawrence Durrell to give him the low-down on it.

D.J. Enright

Where do I find all the time for not reading so many books?

Karl Kraus

There must be five hundred signed copies for particular friends; six for the general public; and one for America.

Oscar Wilde

Literature

I do not want Miss Mannin's feelings to be hurt by the fact that I have never heard of her. At the moment I am debarred from the pleasures of putting her in her place by the fact that she has not got one.

Edith Sitwell

Pope's verses, when they were written, resembled nothing so much as spoonfuls of boiling oil, ladled out by a fiendish monkey at an upstairs window upon such of the passers-by whom the wretch had a grudge against.

Lytton Strachey

The Chronicle of Mites is a mock-heroic poem about the inhabitants of a decaying cheese who speculate about the origin of their species and hold learned discussions upon the meaning of evolution and the Gospel according to Darwin. This cheese-epic is a rather unsavoury production and the style is at times so monstrous and so realistic that the author should be called the Gorgon-Zola of literature.

Oscar Wilde

Except for a sense of humour, Hemingway had everything.

Quentin Crisp

From my close observation of writers, they fall into two groups - those who bleed copiously and visibly at any bad review and those who bleed copiously and secretly at any bad review.

Isaac Asimov

My dog ate *Of Mice and Men* but was unable to finish *Moby Dick*.

George Steinbeck

Literature

The original of Beckford's *Vathek* is not faithful to Henley's translation.

Jorge Luis Borges

Conrad is pretty certain to come back into favour. One of the surest signs of his genius is that women dislike his books.

George Orwell

George Orwell was Don Quixote on a bicycle.

Paul Potts

It seems a great pity they allowed Jane Austen to die a natural death.

Mark Twain

Ten years of rejection slips is nature's way of telling you to stop writing.

Ralph Geiss

We were put to Dickens as children but it never quite took. That unremitting humanity soon had me cheesed off.

Alan Bennett

Somerset Maugham – that old lady is a crashing bore.

Dorothy Parker

I don't think anyone should write their autobiography until after they are dead.

Samuel Goldwyn

Every journalist has a novel in him, which is an excellent place for him to keep it.

Russell Lynes

All the expert help from Earl Mountbatten has not managed to correct Barbara Cartland's apparent belief that Trafalgar came very shortly before Waterloo; perhaps she has confused English history with the London Underground system.

Bernard Levin

Henry James had a mind so fine that no idea could violate it.

T.S. Eliot

You know what would make a good story? Something about a clown who makes people happy, but inside he's real sad. Also, he has severe diarrhea.

Jack Handey

Unprovided with original learning, unfound in the habits of thinking, unskilled in the arts of composition, I resolved to write a book.

Edward Gibbon

I know everything. One has to, to write decently.

Henry James

Cooper's art has some defects. In one place in *Deerslayer*, and in the restricted space of two-thirds of a page, Cooper had scored 114 offences against literary art out of a possible 115. It breaks the record.

Mark Twain

Why was I born with such contemporaries?

Oscar Wilde

An author once told me I must find my muse before I could write. When I finally found her, she was wearing a rubber helmet, a latex catsuit, a very tight corset, and arm binder and ballet-toe boots with seven inch heels. I suspect I am not meant to be a writer.

Ben Salmon

Which of Derrick or Smart is the better poet? Sir, there is no settling the point of precedence between a louse and a flea.

Samuel Johnson

Ideally I'd like to spend two evenings a week talking to Proust and another conversing with the Holy Ghost.

Edna O'Brien

I have written a book entitled 'How to Raise your IQ by Eating Gifted Children'.

Lewis B. Frumkes

Everyone is famous for something, and I am famous for living opposite George Bernard Shaw.

J.M. Barrie

I wrote 'The Name of the Rose' because I felt like poisoning a monk.

Umberto Eco

Literature

Income tax returns are the only imaginative fiction being written today.

Herman Wouk

This is one of those big, fat paperbacks, intended to while away a monsoon or two, which, if thrown with a good overarm action, will bring a water buffalo to its knees.

Nancy Banks-Smith

All I will say about Chesterton is that he likes belching.

George Moore

If Marlowe wrote Shakespeare's works, who wrote Marlowe's?

Woody Allen

Ernest Hemingway was always willing to lend a helping hand to anyone above him.

F. Scott Fitzgerald

I'm writing a book. I've written down all the page numbers and I just have to fill in the rest.

Steven Wright

Is there no beginning to Jeffrey Archer's talent?

Clive Anderson

There seems to be some curious connection between piety and poor rhymes.

Oscar Wilde

A publisher who writes is like a cow in a milk bar.

Arthur Koestler

I am one of the few people outside an institution who can outline the various plots of *Silas Marner*.

W.C. Fields

Alice in Wonderland is nothing but a pack of lies.

Damon Runyon

A thousand naked fornicating couples with their moans and contortions are nothing compared to a good poetic metaphor.

Charles Simic

Anybody who describes his vocation as poet, purveying the modern style of formless verse, is invariably among the meanest and most despicable in the land: vain, empty, conceited, dishonest, dirty, often flea-ridden, and infected by venereal disease, greedy, parasitical, drunken, untruthful, arrogant… all these repulsive qualities, and also irresistibly attractive to women.

Auberon Waugh

His two-line poem is very nice, although there are dull stretches.

Antoine de Rivarol

Thomas Mann's *The Magic Mountain* bids fair to join the list of immortal works of world literature which people bring back from their summer vacations – unread.

Frank D. Hirschback

Literature

Valley of the Dolls is a book for the reader who has put away comic books but isn't ready for editorials in the *Daily News*.

Gloria Steinem

Nobody will make me become an English citizen again. The only possible reason would be for tax reasons.

W.H. Auden

I regard Danielle Steel's *Message from Nam* as a work without any redeeming social value, unless it can be recycled as a cardboard box.

Ellen Goodman

If I had to live my life all over again I would change one thing: I wouldn't read *Moby Dick*.

Woody Allen

My autobiography is a very heavy book which is good because most people read in bed and then doze off. The book will hit them on the head and wake them up again.

Edward Heath

I'm all in favour of keeping dangerous weapons out of the hands of fools. Let's start with typewriters.

Solomon Short

Harold Robbins is able to turn an unplotted unworkable manuscript into an unplotted and unworkable manuscript with lots of sex.

Tom Volpe

I am writing a book on the Crusades, so dull that I can scarcely write it.

Hilaire Belloc

He had been a precocious child. An intellectual. At twelve, he had translated the poems of T.S. Eliot into English.

Woody Allen

When her biographer says of an Italian woman poet, "during some years her Muse was intermitted", we do not wonder at the fact when he casually mentions her ten children.

Anna Spencer

I have read your book and very much like it.

Moses Hadas

Living — Family and Relations

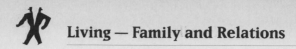

He was an honest man who deserved to live longer; he was intelligent and agreeable, resolute and courageous, to be depended upon, generous and faithful – provided he is really dead.

La Bruyère

If you want to get rid of stinking odours in the kitchen, stop cooking.

Erma Bombeck

I don't know how you feel about old age, but in my case, I didn't even see it coming. It hit me from the rear.

Phyllis Diller

Many are called but few get up.

Oliver Herford

In this world nothing is certain except death and taxes.

Benjamin Franklin

She's the sort of woman who lives for others and you can tell the others by their hunted expression.

C.S. Lewis

An optimist is the kind of person who believes that a housefly is looking for a way out.

George Nathan

The wife was up. I could hear her scraping the toast.

Les Dawson

Cleaning your house while your kids are still growing, is like shovelling the walk before it stops snowing.

Phyllis Diller

In spite of the cost of living, it's still very popular.

Laurence J. Peter

There is only one rule of living – live alone.

Quentin Crisp

The best revenge you can have on intellectuals is to be madly happy.

Albert Camus

The five most terrible words in the English language are 'We've got the builders in'.

Godfrey Smith

Oh, are there two nine o'clocks in the day?

Tallulah Bankhead

I have called my house The Blind Architect.

Spike Milligan

If it weren't for the fact that the TV set and the refrigerator are so far apart, some of us wouldn't get any exercise at all.

Joey Adams

It is better to be rich and healthy than to be poor and sick.

Mark Twain

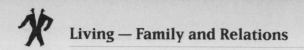

Am I the only person in Britain who was not sexually abused as a child? Every day, I hear adults blaming their dysfunctional personalities on unwanted advances during childhood, yet the bitter truth is that I was a plain boy, and nobody really fancied me. Scout masters, vicars, little old ladies in tea-shops – not one of them offered me so much as a sweetie or muttered, 'It's our little secret', and I've been traumatised ever since by the rejection. And worse, because of their callousness, I'm unable to appear on television, dimly lit and in silhouette, smoking nervously and dumping all my inadequacies on to a long-forgotten grope.

Victor Lewis-Smith

Kids, you tried your best and you failed miserably. The lesson is, never try.

Homer Simpson

I'm not saying I'm old but at my last birthday the candles cost more than the cake.

Bob Hope

It's too bad that whole families have been torn apart by something as simple as wild dogs.

Jack Handey

Don't you hate when your hand falls asleep and you know it will be up all night.

Steven Wright

I don't buy temporary insanity as a murder defence.
Temporary insanity is breaking into someone's home and
ironing all their clothes.

Sue Kolinsky

A child develops individuality long before he develops taste.
I have seen my kids straggle into the kitchen in the morning
with outfits that need only one accessory: an empty gin
bottle.

Erma Bombeck

There is no accounting for tastes, as the woman said when
somebody told her that her son was wanted by the police.

Franklin P. Adams

Parents like the idea of kids, they just don't like their kids.

Morley Saefer

The trick of not working yourself to death is to take a break
as soon as you see a bright light and hear dead relatives
beckon.

Scott Adams

You see more of your children once they leave home.

Lucille Ball

Don't worry about temptation – as you grow older, it starts
avoiding you.

Elbert Hubbard

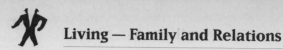

My roommate got a pet elephant. Then it got lost. It's in the apartment somewhere.

Steven Wright

I'm a simple man. All I want is enough sleep for two normal men, enough whiskey for three and enough women for four.

Joel Rosenberg

If the shoe fits – I buy it in every available colour.

Imelda Marcos

I come from a rough neighbourhood. If anyone ever paid their rent, the police immediately came round to see where they got the money from.

Alexei Sayle

Middle age is when you have the choice of two temptations and you choose the one that will get you home earlier.

Edgar Howe

A signature always reveals a man's character – and sometimes even his name.

Evan Esar

I dislike monkeys: they always remind me of my poor relations.

Henry Luttrel

Genius may have its limits, but stupidity is not thus handicapped.

Elbert Hubbard

Sex is something that children never discuss in the presence of their elders.

Arthur Roche

A child of one can be taught not to do certain things such as touch a hot stove, turn on the gas, pull lamps off their tables by their cords, or wake mommy before noon.

Joan Rivers

You know when you're young, you think your dad is Superman. Then you grow up and you realise he's just a regular guy who wears a cape.

Dave Atell

He'd make a lovely corpse.

Charles Dickens

Some men are alive simply because it is against the law to kill them.

Edgar Howe

The moment you're born you're done for.

Arnold Bennett

Life is something that everyone should try at least once.

Henry J. Tillman

Learning to dislike children at an early age saves a lot of expense and aggravation later in life.

Robert Byrne

I am not lost. I am merely locationally challenged.

John M. Ford

I come from a small town where the population never changes. Every time a baby is born some guy immediately leaves town.

Michael Prichard

Barnum was wrong – it's more like every thirty seconds.

Eric Moore

My mother used to say there are no strangers, only friends you haven't met yet. She's now in a maximum security twilight home in Australia.

Edna Everage

I like life – it gives you something to do.

Ronnie Shakes

It is hard to disguise your feelings when you put a lot of relatives on the train for home.

Edgar Howe

A perfume is any smell that is used to drown a worse one.

Elbert Hubbard

Anyone who uses the phrase 'easy as taking candy from a baby' has never tried taking candy from a baby.

Fran Lebowitz

I have noticed your hostility towards him. I ought to have guessed you were friends.

Malcolm Bradbury

A sobering thought: what if, at this very moment I am living up to my full potential?

Jane Wagner

When you are down and out, something always turns up, usually the noses of your friends.

Orson Welles

Have you ever noticed that on those rare occasions when you do need turpentine, the can, which you bought in 1978, and have been moving from household to household ever since, is always empty?

Dave Barry

Laziness is nothing more than resting before you get tired.

Jules Renard

You have to get up early if you want to get out of bed.

Groucho Marx

Ambition is a poor excuse for not having sense enough to be lazy.

Charlie McCarthy

There was a time when father amounted to something in the United States. He was held with some esteem in the community; he had some authority in his own household; his views were sometimes taken seriously by his children; and even his wife paid heed to him from time to time.

Adlai Stevenson

When the Black Camel comes for me, I am not going to go kicking and screaming. I am, however, going to try to talk my way out of it. 'No, no, you want the other Walter Slovotsky.'

Walter Slovotsky

An eternity with Beelzebub and all his hellish instruments of death shall be a picnic compared to five minutes with me and this pencil.

Rowan Atkinson

If you're a really good kid, I'll give you a ride on a buzz-saw.

W.C. Fields

Children are natural mimics who act like their parents, despite every effort to teach them good manners.

P.J. O'Rourke

When your mother asks, 'Do you want a piece of advice?' it's a mere formality. It doesn't matter if you answer yes or no. You're going to get it anyway.

Erma Bombeck

Douglas Fairbanks has always faced a situation in the only way he knew how, by running away from it.

Mary Pickford

If paternity leave was granted it would result in a direct incitement to a population explosion.

Ian Gow

You can calculate Zsa Zsa Gabor's age by the rings on her fingers.

Bob Hope

Bring the little ones to me and I will get a good price for them.

Eugene Fegg

How little it takes to make life unbearable: a pebble in the shoe, a cockroach in the spaghetti, a woman's laugh.

H.L. Mencken

Times were tough when I was a child but they were tough for everyone. If you wanted a new pair of shoes, you went to the baths on a Saturday night.

Tommy Docherty

I have been trying for some time to develop a lifestyle that doesn't require my presence.

Gary Trudeau

Threescore years and ten are enough; if a man can't suffer all the misery he wants in that time, he must be numb.

Josh Billings

I have no mother sir — someone interfered with my aunt.

Nicholas Jones

We are born naked, wet, and hungry. Then things get worse.

W.C. Fields

I come from a stupid family. During the Civil War my great uncle fought for the west.

Rodney Dangerfield

I once met a suicidal identical twin who killed his brother by mistake.

Steven Wright

I intend to live forever; so far, so good.

Steven Wright

I'm as confused as a baby in a topless bar.

Robin Williams

I used to look like this when I was young and now I still do.

Yogi Berra

I buy life insurance year after year but I've never been lucky yet.

Henny Youngman

My young brother asked me what happens after we die. I told him we get buried under the earth and the worms eat our bodies. I guess I should have told him the truth – that most of us go to hell and burn eternally, but I didn't want to upset him.

Emo Philips

The death of Francis Macomber was a turning point in his life.

Richard Lederer

Happiness is the moment when you get out of your corsets at night.

Joyce Grenfell

Time and tide wait for no man, but time always stands still for a woman of thirty.

Robert Frost

I am always pleased to see my friends, happy to be with my wife and family, but the high-spot of every day is when I first catch a glimpse of myself in the shaving mirror.

Robert Morley

My family was so poor that my brother was made in
Hong Kong.

Jim Davidson

When they asked Jack Benny to do something for the
Actors' Orphanage – he shot both his parents and moved in.

Bob Hope

My father carries around the picture of the kid who came
with his wallet.

Rodney Dangerfield

My kids have always perceived the bathroom as a place you
can wait it out until all the groceries are unloaded from the
car.

Erma Bombeck

I bought a self-help tape called 'How to Handle
Disappointment'. When I got it home the box was empty.

Jonathan Droll

We all tend to idealise tolerance, then wonder why we find
ourselves infested with losers and nut cases.

Patrick Hayden

He was either a man of about a hundred and fifty who was
rather young for his years, or a man of about a hundred and
ten who had been aged by trouble.

P.G. Wodehouse

Body piercing is a powerful, compelling visual statement that says, 'Gee, in today's competitive job market, what can I do to make myself less employable?'

Dennis Miller

All the good things in life are immoral, illegal or heavily taxed.

Oscar Wilde

I am happiest when I am idle. I could live for months without performing any kind of labour, and at the expiration of that time I should feel fresh and vigorous enough to go right on in the same way for numerous more months.

Artemus Ward

Housework can't kill you, but why take a chance?

Phyllis Diller

Why do women of sixty want to have babies? So they can both be in nappies at the same time?

Patrick Murray

I wasn't born in a slum, but my family moved into one as soon as they could afford it.

Melville Landon

My mother had morning sickness *after* I was born.

Rodney Dangerfield

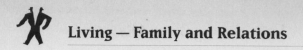

My mum and dad are both dead and now I think of some of the things I wish I'd said to them, like 'be careful of that bus'.
Kevin Gildea

Veni, Vidi, Visa (We came, we saw, we went shopping).
Jan Barrett

They said Beethoven was mad; they said Einstein was mad; they said Louis was mad – Louis was my uncle, he was mad.
Jimmy Durante

A boy's best friend is his mother.
Norman Bates

A father is a quartermaster and emissary of subsistence provided by nature for our maintenance in the period before we have learned to live by prey.
Ambrose Bierce

More boys would follow in their father's footsteps if they weren't afraid of getting caught.
E. C. McKenzie

There is nobody, absolutely nobody, who is thirstier than a four-year-old who has just gone to bed.
Fran Lebowitz

My mother put up a Jewish satellite dish – it just picks up the problems from other families.
Richard Lewis

The moment I stepped outside my mother's womb, I realised I had made a mistake.

Quentin Crisp

It's easy to be happy in life if your one concern is wondering how much saliva to dribble.

Woody Allen

When I come back in the next life, I want to come back as a golf pro's wife. She wakes up every morning at the crack of ten and is faced by her first major decision of the day: whether to have breakfast in bed or in the hotel coffee shop.

Don Sikes

We weren't hoping for a boy or a girl, we were just happy to take pot luck.

Steve Davis

Anything dropped in the bathroom falls into the toilet.

Paul Sloane

A coin, sleeve-button or a collar-button dropped in a bedroom will hide itself and be hard to find. A handkerchief in bed can't be found.

Mark Twain

The worst waste of breath, next to playing the saxaphone, is advising a son.

Kin Hubbard

Whosoever shall not fall by the sword or by famine shall fall by pestilence, so why bother shaving?

Woody Allen

Practically everyone but myself is a pusillanimous son of a bitch.

George Patton

Any amusing deaths recently?

Maurice Bowra

There were twenty kids in our family. You didn't dare put your tongue out or someone would stick a fork in it.

Roy Brown

The little trouble in the world that is not due to love is due to friendship.

Edgar Howe

I remember the time I was kidnapped and they sent back a piece of my finger to my father. He said he wanted more proof.

Rodney Dangerfield

I am beginning to understand those animals you read about where the mother has got to hide the young so the father won't eat them.

W.C. Fields

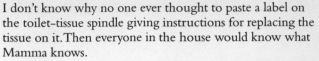

I don't know why no one ever thought to paste a label on the toilet-tissue spindle giving instructions for replacing the tissue on it. Then everyone in the house would know what Mamma knows.

Erma Bombeck

If nobody said anything unless he knew what he was talking about, a ghastly hush would descend upon the earth.

A. P. Herbert

Most men never mature; they simply grow taller.

Leo Rosten

I think it's wonderful you could all be here to celebrate the forty-third anniversary of my thirty-ninth birthday. We decided not to light any candles this year — we were afraid Pan Am would mistake it for a runway.

George Burns

My aunt died at precisely 10:47 am and the old grandfather clock stopped precisely at this moment also. It fell on her.

Paul Merton

If you take the path less travelled maybe it's because you march to the beat of a different drum. On the other hand maybe you're just completely lost.

Patrick Murray

I know when I'm going to die because my birth certificate has an expiration date on it.

Steven Wright

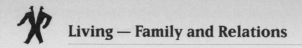

Never knock on Death's door. Ring the bell and run away. Death really hates that.

Matt Frewer

Few parents nowadays pay any regard to what their children say to them. The old fashioned respect for the young is fast dying out.

OscarWilde

I was upstairs painting a bedroom when I felt hungry, so I picked up the telephone and had the Post Office deliver a telegram to my wife downstairs asking her to send up some soup and sandwiches.

Spike Milligan

When your mom is mad with your dad, don't let her brush your hair.

Jean Kerr

You know you're getting old; there are certain signs. I walked past a cemetery and two guys ran after me with shovels.

Rodney Dangerfield

The last time I saw my mother-in-law, she was climbing the Empire State Building with King Kong in her mouth.

John Arnold

My parents have been visiting me for a few days. I just dropped them off at the airport. They leave tomorrow.

Margaret Smith

The trouble with children is that they are not returnable.

Quentin Crisp

Estimated from his wife's experience, the average man spends fully one quarter of his life in looking for his shoes.

Helen Rowland

My friend has a baby. I'm writing down all the noises he makes so later I can ask him what he meant.

Steven Wright

Now they show you how detergents take out bloodstains, a pretty violent image there. I think if you've got a T-shirt with a bloodstain all over it, maybe laundry isn't your biggest problem. Maybe you should get rid of the body before you do the wash.

Jerry Seinfeld

I wouldn't mind dying – it's that business of having to stay dead that scares the hell out of me.

Ralph Geiss

My theory on housework is, if the item doesn't multiply, smell, catch fire or block the refrigerator door, let it be. No one cares. Why should you?

Erma Bombeck

The way of the transgessor is hard because it's so crowded.

Kin Hubbard

Living — Family and Relations

No matter how old a mother is, she watches her middle-aged childre for signs of improvement.

Florida Scott-Maxwell

Man invented language to satisfy his deep need to complain.

Lily Tomlin

Parents say things like 'Would you like a smack?' and 'I'll teach you to be disobedient'.

Dave Allen

Princess Michael of Kent?
Far too grand for the likes of us, dear!

Queen Elizabeth II

Love, Sex, Marriage, Men and Women

I like younger women. Their stories are shorter.

Tom McGuane

The only thing my husband and I have in common is that we were married on the same day.

Phyllis Diller

I don't know what the Left is doing, said the Right Hand, but it looks fascinating.

James Broughton

I bequeath to my wife the sum of one shilling for a tram fare so she can go somewhere and drown herself.

Francis Lord

Where did I first kiss my present partner? On her insistence.

Daire O'Brien

I used to be Snow White, but I drifted.

Mae West

I haven't spoken to my wife for over a month. We haven't had a row – it's just that I'm afraid to interrupt her.

Les Dawson

I dislike the idea of wives about a house: they accumulate dust. Besides, so few of the really nice women in my set could afford to marry me.

H.H. Munro

One hard and fast rule of my sex life is only one willy in the bed at a time.

A.A. Gill

Most women are not so young as they are painted.

Max Beerbohm

All that this humourless document, the Kinsey Report, proves is:
(a) that all men lie when they are asked about their adventures in amour, and
(b) that pedagogues are singly naïve and credulous creatures.

H.L. Mencken

Every time Magda Goebbels saw Hitler, her ovaries rattled.

Peter Watson

Never try to impress a woman: because if you do she'll expect you to keep up the standard for the rest of your life. And the pace, my friends, is devastating.

W.C. Fields

If a woman has had more than three husbands, she poisons them; avoid her.

William Maguire

The only time a woman really succeeds in changing a man is when he is a baby.

Natalie Wood

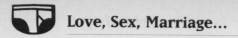

If a tree falls in the woods and there is nobody there to hear it fall, does it still make a sound? And if a man speaks and there is no woman there to correct him, is he still wrong?

Camille Paglia

I'm too shy to express my sexual needs except over the phone to people I don't know.

Gary Shandling

Women should never wear anything that panics the cat.

P.J. O'Rourke

Lord Ormsby 85 has just married Lady Astorite 18. The groom's gift to the bride was an antique pendant.

Peter Shaw

Did I sleep with her? Not a wink, father, not a wink.

Brendan Behan

When men are angry and upset, they rebel by hurting others; when women are angry and upset, they rebel by hurting themselves: bulimia, anorexia, self-mutilation, suicide, getting married to members of the Windsor family.

Julie Burchill

A bridegroom is a man who has spent a lot of money on a suit that no one notices.

Josh Billings

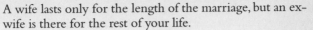

A wife lasts only for the length of the marriage, but an ex-wife is there for the rest of your life.

Jim Samuels

I have difficulty in avoiding the persistent attentions of ladies of the street. It's a case of the tail dogging the wag.

S. J. Perelman

Have the florist send some roses to Mrs Upjohn and write, 'Emily, I love you', on the back of the bill'.

Groucho Marx

When widows exclaim loudly against second marriages, I would always lay a wager, that the man, if not the wedding-day is absolutely fixed upon.

Henry Fielding

I can honestly say that I always look on Pauline as one of the nicest girls I was ever engaged to.

P. G. Wodehouse

Only one man in a thousand is a leader of men – the other nine hundred and ninety-nine follow women.

Groucho Marx

The purpose of sexual intercourse is to get it over with as long as possible.

Steven Max Singer

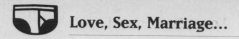

A woman who takes her husband about with her everywhere is like a cat that goes on playing with a mouse long after she's killed it.

H.H. Munro

It is only rarely that one can see in a little boy the promise of a man, but one can almost always see in a little girl the threat of a woman.

Alexandre Dumas

The proliferation of massage establishments in London in the last few years appears to indicate a dramatic increase in muscular disorders amongst the male population.

Evelyn Waugh

I have such poor vision I can date anybody.

Gary Shandling

I would go out with women my age, but there are no women my age.

George Burns

In biblical times, a man could have as many wives as he could afford. Just like today.

Abigail Van Buren

I don't know how much it costs to get married – I'm still paying for it.

Les Dawson

God gave men a penis and a brain, but not enough blood to use both at the same time.

Robin Williams

A married couple playing cards together is just a fight that hasn't started yet.

George Burns

The feller that puts off marrying until he can support a wife ain't much in love.

Kin Hubbard

Guns don't kill people; husbands that come home early kill people.

Don Rose

I once placed an ad in the personal columns of *Private Eye* saying that I wanted to meet a rich well-insured widow with a view to murdering her. I got 48 replies.

Spike Milligan

I am not against hasty marriages, where a mutual flame is fanned by an adequate income.

Wilkie Collins

They say that the daughter-in-law of the Spanish Ambassador is not ugly, and has as good a set of teeth as one can have, when one has but two and those black.

Horace Walpole

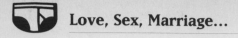

I bank at this women's bank. Everybody is in the red three or four days a month.

Judith Carter

I haven't had any open marriages, though quite a few have been ajar.

Zsa Zsa Gabor

The most romantic thing any woman ever said to me in bed was 'Are you sure you're not a cop?'

Larry Brown

As Major Denis Bloodnok exclaimed when told there were only two sexes: 'It's not enough, I say'.

Albert Hall

Fat generally tends to make a man a better husband. His wife is happy in the knowledge she is not married to a woman chaser. Few fat men chase girls, because they get winded so easily.

Hal Boyle

It wasn't exactly a divorce – I was traded.

Tim Conway

By love, of course, I refer to romantic love – the love between man and woman, rather than between mother and child, or a boy and his dog, or two headwaiters.

Woody Allen

I have little experience of marriage, having been married only once.

Oscar Wilde

There is a way of transferring funds that is even faster than electronic banking. It's called marriage.

James McGavran

If you have to ask if somebody is male or female, don't.

Patrick Murray

Transsexuals always seem to feel that they have been Shirley Bassey trapped inside a man's body rather than an assistant from an Oxfam Shop trapped inside a man's body.

Paul Hoggart

I require only three things of a man. He must be handsome, ruthless and stupid.

Dorothy Parker

I told him that I would give him a call but what I really meant was that I would rather have my nipples torn off by wild dogs than see him again.

Rita Rudner

Men are people, just like women.

Fenella Fielding

What attracted me to Lytton in the first place was his knees.

Carrington Strachey

If a woman hasn't met the right man by the time she's twenty-four, she may be lucky.

Deborah Kerr

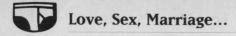 **Love, Sex, Marriage...**

You remember your first mountain in much the same way as you remember having your first sexual experience, except that climbing doesn't make as much mess and you don't cry for a week if Ben Nevis forgets to phone the next morning.

Muriel Gray

A woman will lie about anything, just to stay in practice.

Phillip Marlowe

She was the finest woman that ever walked the streets.

Mae West

When women are depressed they either eat or go shopping. Men invade another country.

Elayne Boosler

Love is the one game that is never called off on account of darkness.

Tom Masson

It is better taste somehow that a man should be unfaithful to his wife away from home.

Barbara Pym

Advice to young men about to marry – don't.

Mister Punch

Bigamy is one way of avoiding the painful publicity of divorce and the expense of alimony.

Oliver Herford

Women – you can't live with them and you can't live with them.

Marsh Mellow

Amnesia is a condition that enables a woman who has gone through labour to have sex again.

Fran Lebowitz

You're so gorgeous, I bet even the bags under your eyes are made by Gucci.

Kenny Everett

My girlfriend tells me I'm a pearl – the result of constant irritation.

Jim Davis

Norman Mailer likes women so much he even likes Hillary Clinton.

Paul Johnson

No one will ever win the battle of the sexes; there's too much fraternising with the enemy.

Henry Kissinger

Dickie Mountbatten loved to look at the menu, but rarely ate the main course.

Douglas Fairbanks Jr.

Some people are just not cut out to be married – like men.

Jimmy Tarbuck

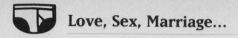

I saw this nature show on TV about how the male elk douses himself with urine to smell sweeter to the opposite sex. What a coincidence.

Jack Handey

O what a tangled web we weave when first we practice to conceive.

Don Herold

I don't think their marriage will last. When the groom said 'I do', the bride said 'Don't use that tone of voice with me'.

Gary Apple

She didn't mean to get pregnant. It was a cock-up.

Roger Kilroy-Silk

Since I met my new girlfriend I can't eat, drink or sleep. I'm broke.

Rick Nelson

At first I thought he was walking a dog. Then I realised it was his date.

Edith Massey

One advantage of being pregnant is that you don't have to worry about getting pregnant.

Peter Nicholls

One night Mr and Mrs Reginald Bingham went to Ciro's. They had been married only about six months. Mr Bingham had never been to Ciro's before in his life. His surprise, therefore, upon seeing his wife there, was considerable.

Ben Travers

I went to a discount massage parlour the other night – it was self service.

Rodney Dangerfield

I am one of the few males who suffers from penis envy.

Woody Allen

If treated properly sex can be the most beautiful thing in the world.

Elizabeth Taylor

I believe in clubs for women – but only if every other form of persuasion fails.

W.C. Fields

A man always remembers his first love with special tenderness, but after that he begins to bunch them.

H.L. Mencken

All men are mortal. Socrates was mortal. Therefore, all men are Socrates. Which means that all men are homosexuals.

Woody Allen

I look like an elderly wasp in an interesting condition.

Mrs Patrick Campbell

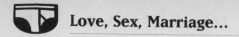

Sex and death, two things that come once in a lifetime. Only after death you're not nauseous.

Woody Allen

PMS means never wanting to say you're sorry.

Diana Jordan

One of the best things about marriage is that it gets young people to bed at a decent hour.

M.M. Musselman

Our union has been blessed with issues.

Peter De Vries

Oh God, in the name of Thine only beloved Son, Jesus Christ, Our Lord, let him phone me now.

Dorothy Parker

My wife told me her waters had just gone so I told her not to worry that I would get her some more.

Dave Barry

A husband is what is left of a lover after the nerve has been extracted.

Helen Rowland

The first time Adam had the chance, he put the blame on a woman.

Nancy Astor

If you let women have their way, you will generally get even with them in the end.

Will Rogers

So far as is known, no widow has ever eloped.

E. W. Howe

I think it's a great idea to talk during sex as long as it's about snooker.

Steve Davis

She was a classy girl – she smoked a fifty-cent cigar.

W.C. Fields

I have got little feet because nothing grows in the shade.

Dolly Parton

Women represent the triumph of matter over mind, just as men represent the triumph of mind over morals.

Oscar Wilde

The happiness of a married man depends on the people he has not married.

Oscar Wilde

Women delight in men over seventy. They offer one the devotion of a lifetime.

Oscar Wilde

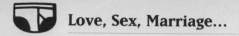

If little green men land in your back yard, hide any little green women you've got in the house.

Mike Harding

I used to be with three women until 5 a.m. Now I'm in training, it's five women until 3 a.m.

Alberto Tomba

My wife has helped me considerably with my career. Late one night in 1924 we got home from somewhere and I said I was hungry, so she gave me a verbal picture of the location of the pantry.

Ring Lardner

Men are creatures with two legs and eight hands.

Jayne Mansfield

Hollywood divorces cost so much because they're worth it.

Johnny Carson

A lot of women complain about periods but I don't because I think they're brilliant. Especially if you know somebody who lives next door who you can't stand who's got a white sofa.

Jo Brand

The other night I said to my wife, 'Do you feel that the excitement has gone out of our marriage?' She said, 'I'll discuss it with you during the next commercial'.

Milton Berle

This 'relationship' business is one big waste of time. It is just Mother Nature urging you to breed, breed, breed. Learn from nature. Learn from our friend the spider. Just mate once and then kill him.

Ruby Wax

They buried the hatchet, but in a shallow well-marked grave.

Dorothy Walworth

I'd love to go out with you, but my favourite commercial is on TV.

Rita Rudner

I blame myself for my boyfriend's death. I shot him.

Jo Brand

The real drawback to marriage is that it makes one unselfish. And unselfish people are colourless.

Oscar Wilde

She had so many gold teeth she used to have to sleep with her head in a safe.

W.C. Fields

My wife will buy anything marked down. Last week she brought home an escalator.

Henny Youngman

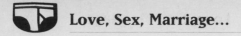

Sometimes a man just can't satisfy all of a woman's desires.
Which is why God invented dental floss.

Susanne Kollrack

I sometimes wonder whether all the female nudity you see
in newspapers and magazines may not reflect a certain
wistfulness for the days when men and women were more
easily told apart.

Evelyn Waugh

Among these Mr Quiverful, the rector of Puddingdale,
whose wife still continued to present him from year to year
with fresh pledges of her love.

Anthony Trollope

Please God, keep me from telephoning him, please God.

Dorothy Parker

Bestiality is a poke in a pig.

Andrew Austin

I've never been married, but I tell people I'm divorced so
they won't think something is wrong with me.

Elayne Boosler

To attract men, I wear a perfume called 'new car interior'.

Rita Rudner

I'm looking for Miss Right, or at least Miss Right Now.

Robin Williams

I'd love to go out with you, but I want to spend more time with my blender.

Rita Rudner

My husbands have been very unlucky.

Lucrezia Borgia

Media and Films

Talent is sometimes forgiven in Hollywood, genius never.
Evelyn Waugh

The Antiques Roadshow now becomes the For God's Sake
Stop Telling me How Rare and Delightful This Heirloom Is
I just want to hear how much it's worth and even though I'll
tell you that I'll never sell it because it has sentimental value
as soon as the show finishes I'll shoot off to Sothebys and
flog it and blow the lot on a fortnight in Majorca Show.
Victor Lewis-Smith

Well if I dialled a wrong number, why did you answer the
phone?
James Thurber

Leonardo DiCaprio is patently the result of an unnatural act
of passion between William Hague and the piglet from Babe.
A.A. Gill

They used to shoot Shirley Temple through gauze. They
ought to shoot me through linoleum.
Tallulah Bankhead

It is part of the social mission of every great newspaper to
provide a refuge and a home for the largest possible number
of salaried eccentrics.
Roy Thomson

Whom is fooling whom?
Joan Crawford

The voice-over narration on this movie helps to explain what is going on, and became necessary when the producers lost the soundtrack.

Christopher Tookey

For those of you watching who haven't got TV sets, live commentary is on Radio Two.

David Coleman

It's Norden, Speight and Sykes, back from the dead, for one night only.

Spike Milligan

Lillian Hellman is deceased but in need of further persecution.

Paul Kirchner

Find out what those people pushing an elephant along the corridor of the twentieth floor of the New Yorker are doing, but don't tell me.

Alexander Woollcott

Good news is no news.

Kirk Douglas

At the movie my tears stuck in their little ducts, refusing to be jerked.

Peter Stack

Television has raised writing to a new low.

Samuel Goldwyn

I'm here to speak about Kirk Douglas's wit, his charm, his warmth, his talent – at last a real acting job!

Burt Lancaster

There are two continuity announcements guaranteed to make the viewer's blood run cold – 'and the programme is introduced by Ross King' along with 'This programme was originally transmitted by BBC East Midlands'.

Victor Lewis-Smith

Michael Jackson was a poor black boy who grew up to be a rich white woman.

Molly Ivins

I wonder if Steve McQueen made that movie before or after he died.

Yogi Berra

Blind Date tempts our voyeuristic appetites, although what everybody really wants to see would required infra-red cameras and a team from the BBC Badger Watch Unit.

Victor Lewis-Smith

The magician Joe Pasguale did something Paul Daniels can't do – he pulled at the roots of his hair.

Victor Lewis-Smith

I don't care if the movie doesn't make a nickel, I just want every man, woman, and child in America to see it.

Samuel Goldwyn

I had no idea that the Academy Awards were televised. Boy, is my face red.

David Letterman

An acquaintance of mine, who once spent several months in a psychiatric hospital, remembers a curious fact about the television set there. It was permanently turned to ITV, with tape stuck over the selection buttons and he had to apply for a special chit to watch any other channel.

Victor Lewis-Smith

In *Lawrence of Arabia* they got only two things right – the camels and the sand.

Lowell Thomas

Wilcox's film ended up like a convincing advertisement for euthanasia. Desmond Wilcox is married to Esther Rantzen and has been for a very long time.

A.A. Gill

The biggest hit movie in Russia is *Escape to Alcatraz*.

Leo Rosten

Hurry Sundown is perhaps the worst-reviewed film of all time. *At Long Last Love* must run it close, but the extra ingredients of racial offensiveness and juvenile smut give this one the edge.

Christopher Tookey

Teen Angel had all the usual ingredients: boy meets girl; girl stalls her car on railway tracks and picks this inopportune moment to search for her boyfriend's missing school ring; girl is crushed to death by a moving train.

Karl Shaw

The telephone is a good way to talk to people without having to offer them a drink.

Fran Lebowitz

So they are going to show a man die on television; after Barry Norman, I don't think I could sit through it again.

A.A. Gill

The human race is faced with a cruel choice – work or daytime television.

Dave Barry

The advertisements are the most truthful part of a newspaper.

Thomas Jefferson

The end of each commercial break was coming like the next wave of peristalsis during a night of vomiting, that Oh-God-it's-starting-again feeling.

Victor Lewis-Smith

To criticise Hurry Sundown would be like tripping a dwarf.

Wilfrid Sheed

Media and Films

Watching John Thaw is like being embalmed alive by an arthritic with halitosis.

A.A. Gill

For extra fun, play with the colour control until I turn green.

Dave Letterman

Television is a kind of radio which lets people at home see what the studio audience is not laughing at.

Fred Allen

Desk-top publishing is a system of software and hardware enabling users to create documents with a cornucopia of typefaces and graphics and the intellectual content of a Formica slab.

Stephen Manes

Even when James Stewart made a visible effort to play a love scene, he always gave the impression he was wearing only one shoe and looking for the other while he slowly droned his lines.

Marlene Dietrich

Gentlemen, listen to me slowly.

Samuel Goldwyn

Hollywood is a place where they place you under contract instead of under observation.

Walter Winchell

Marilyn Monroe has breasts of granite and a mind like
Gruyere cheese.

Billy Wilder

Publishing is harder to get into than the inner rectum of the
Vatican.

Gerard Kelly

When I was presenting *Cluedo* on television, we used to have
to turn over the studio audience in case they got bed sores.

Chris Tarrant

Don't you wish there was a knob on the TV to turn up the
intelligence? There's one called 'Brightness' but doesn't
work.

Tom Gallagher

The fact that a man is a newspaper reporter is evidence of
some flaw of character.

Lyndon B. Johnson

The ideal voice for radio may be defined as having no
substance, no sex, no owner, and a message of importance for
every housewife.

Harry Wade

For this scene let's get some Indians from the reservoir.

Samuel Goldwyn

Compared to Hale and Pace, everything on television deserves a BAFTA.

A.A. Gill

The ad in the paper said 'Big Sale. Last Week!' Why advertise? I already missed it. They're just rubbing it in.

Yakov Smirnoff

I won't believe in colour television until I see it in black and white.

Samuel Goldwyn

Arnold Schwarzenegger looks like a condom full of walnuts.

Clive James

I never go to movies where the hero's bust is bigger than the heroine's.

Groucho Marx

Clark Gable's ears made him look like a taxicab with both doors open.

Howard Hughes

I can't honestly say that Esther Williams ever acted in an Andy Hardy picture, but she swam in one.

Mickey Rooney

If Cubby Broccoli were on fire, I wouldn't piss on him to put out the flames.

Sean Connery

I think we must re-evaluate what we mean by quality on
television.

Catherine Everett

Who picks David Letterman's clothes – Stevie Wonder?
Don Rickles

I'm No 10 at the box office. Right under Barbara Streisand.
Can you imagine being under Barbara Streisand? Get me a
bag, I may throw up.

Walter Matthau

Film-making is a team effort. My idea of a team effort is
sixty people doing exactly what I tell them.

Michael Winner

The most notorious hiccup with the new digital technology
was when Radio Four's *Today* programme broadcast
Mongolian throat singing instead of Tony Benn's thoughts
on US missile strikes.

Carol Midgley

The official movie ratings are 'General', 'Parental Guidance',
and 'Restricted', I have my own ratings. They are 'See at
Movie Theatre', 'Wait for video', and 'Not even if when it
Comes on Cable Someone Comes to My House and Staples
My Eyes Open'.

Rita Rudner

Media and Films

I am not a dirty old man. I may be dirty but I'm not old.

Russ Meyer

In Hollywood they knew only one word of more than one syllable, and that is "fillum".

Louis Sherwin

Gina Lollobrigida? I never criticise my elders.

Sophia Loren

Spielberg isn't a filmmaker, he's a confectioner.

Alex Cox

An amateur thinks it's funny if you dress a man up as an old lady, put him in a wheelchair and give the wheelchair a push that sends it spinning down a slope towards a wall. For a pro, it's got to be a real old lady.

Groucho Marx

Bob Hoskins is just a testicle with legs.

Pauline Kael

The main amusement in watching *Bonfire of the Vanities* is to be had from watching Melaine Griffith's breasts which change size quite dramatically and without warning (she had implants during the shooting).

Christopher Tookey

Here's something to think about: how come you never see a headline like PSYCHIC WINS LOTTERY?

Steven Wright

Media and Films

Do you know what are making headlines at the moment?
Corduroy pillows.

Steven Wright

Standing downwind, Robert Mitchum is probably the
sexiest guy going today.

Joan Rivers

Walter Matthau looked like a half-melted rubber bulldog.

John Simon

Steven Spielberg always wanted to be a little boy when he
grew up.

Rainer Fassbinder

When confronted by a difficult problem, you can solve it
more easily by reducing it to the question, "How would the
Lone Ranger have handled this?"

Phil Brady

I used to be a proofreader for a skywriting company.

Steven Wright

The atmosphere of the BBC is something halfway between a
girl's school and a lunatic asylum.

George Orwell

James Lane and Donald Jones couldn't direct lemmings off a
cliff.

Doug Brod

I admit I've never seen the point of Hale and Pace. And I can't get close to the faintest inkling of why anybody would want to write, produce or, worse, transmit this show, unless of course compromising photographs, threats of extreme violence to children and cocaine and sex were involved at the planning stage.

A.A. Gill

If you don't disagree with me, how will I know I'm right?

Samuel Goldwyn

O.K. O.K. so in the novel they are lesbians. In the movie we can make them Americans.

Samuel Goldwyn

What makes a good movie? Ordinary rape and murder just don't make it any more. It's much better to have ultra-violence, chainsaw massacres, X-rated Draculas, and continents sinking into the sea with the entire population lost, at the very least.

Jon Davidson

The TV presenter described me in a national newspaper as the living person she most despised and suggested I was obnoxious, repellent and impotent. I sent her a polaroid of myself in full fumescence and have heard nothing since.

Victor Lewis-Smith

Medicine and Doctors

Medicine and Doctors

Lassa Fever is so bad it makes spending one's entire life in Bognor Regis look good.

George Thomas

When I was young I was so mixed up my parents sent me to a child psychiatrist. But the boy was useless.

Rodney Dangerfield

Are you all right? You should have two of everything down the sides and one of everything down the middle.

Ken Dodd

Jonathan Miller has put his finger on it – it's OK, he's a doctor, he's allowed to put his finger on it.

Victor Lewis-Smith

I told my doctor I get very tired when I go on a diet, so he gave me pep pills. Know what happened? I ate faster.

Joe E. Lewis

I've decided that perhaps I'm bulimic and just keep forgetting to purge.

Paula Poundstone

Every man has a sane spot somewhere.

Robert Louis Stevenson

God heals, and the doctor takes the fee.

Benjamin Franklin

Here is a test to see if you are obese. Do people sometimes use you to show their home-movies on?

Lee Schreiner

Then Norm went and died. I could have given up and returned to Australia – that brown and pleasant land, but instead I founded the charity Friends of the Prostate, to increase knowledge of the Cinderella organ.

Edna Everage

To avoid dandruff falling on your shoulders, step nimbly to one side.

George Burns

When Charles II had a fit while shaving in 1685, he was lucky to be treated with the finest medical advice of the day. He was attended by 14 physicians who drew blood, forced him to vomit violently and gave him a strong laxative. Then they shaved his head, applied blistering agents to his scalp, put special plasters made from pigeon droppings onto the soles of this feet, fed him bezoar stones (much – prized gallstones from the bladder of a goat) and made him drink 40 drops of extract from a dead man's skull. He died two days later.

Karl Shaw

Akenesia is a medical term to denote the absence of kinesia.

Lee Schreiner

I'm going to Boston to see my doctor. He's a very sick man.

Fred Allen

I believe that Traill is ill. Nothing trivial I hope.

John P. Mahaffy

Varicose veins are the result of an improper selection of grandparents.

William Osler

Dad always thought laughter was the best medicine, which I guess is why several of us died of tuberculosis.

Jack Handey

A reputable optometrist is one who does not make you remove your clothes for the examination.

George Thomas

In Govan, until something actually turns black and drops off, they think it's bad form to bother the doctor.

Rab. C. Nesbitt

The lungs are the largest organs in the body, and with good reason. They are essential to three of the hypochondriac's most vital bodily functions – coughing, wheezing and smoking.

George Thomas

Servants should not be ill. We have quite enough illnesses of our own without them adding to the symptoms.

Diana Cooper

Medicine and Doctors

In the middle ages, people took potions for their ailments.
In the 19th century they took snake oil. Citizens of today's
shiny technological age are too modern for that. They take
antioxidants and extract of cactus instead.

Charles Krauthammer

Robert Lister, described as "the finest surgeon in Europe",
had a personal best of 28 seconds for a leg amputation,
although while achieving this record he accidentally cut of
two of his assistant's fingers and the patient's left testicle.

Karl Shaw

After five days in hospital, I took a turn for the nurse.

Spike Milligan

Get your room full of good air, then shut up the windows
and keep it. It will last for years. Anyway, don't keep using
your lungs all the time. Let them rest.

Stephen Leacock

The true aim of medicine is to rescue men from the
consequences of their vices.

H.L. Mencken

The cervix is an anatomical term referring to either the
opening of the uterus or to the bones of the neck – an
unfortunate ambiguity that has resulted in several famous
operating theatre errors.

George Thomas

A hospital is no place to be sick.

Samuel Goldwyn

Medicine and Doctors

Ken Dodd went in for open-heart surgery. They opened him up and found another forty grand.

Jimmy Tarbuck

It is no longer a question of staying healthy. It's a question of finding a sickness you like.

Jackie Mason

I told my doctor I broke my leg in two places. He told me to quit going to those places.

Henny Youngman

For many years I believed an innuendo was an Italian suppository.

Spike Milligan

An autopsy is a diagnostic procedure by which a hypochondriac hopes for vindication.

George Thomas

There are men who would be afraid to commit themselves even on the doctrine that castor oil is a laxative.

Camille Flammanion

Psychoanalysis is spending forty dollars an hour to squeal on your mother.

Mike Connolly

God put the waterworks too close to the playground.

Lee Schreiner

A doctor's reputation is made by the number of eminent men who die under his care.

George Bernard Shaw

Half of the modern drugs could well be thrown out of the window, except that the birds might eat them.

Martin Fischer

The one glaring design fault of the National Health Service is that it keeps old gits above ground well beyond their sell-by date.

A.A. Gill

Arthur Skelton was known as 'The Pox Doctor's Clerk'. I don't think he did actually ever render clerical assistance to a genito-urinary specialist, but he had one of those unfortunate faces that made you think he might have.

Jeffrey Bernard

She not only kept her lovely figure, she's added so much to it.

Bob Fosse

I think my mum was a plastic surgeon – she used to say to me 'I'll put that smile on the other side of your face'.

Mick Mulcahy

When I was born the doctor came out to the waiting room and said 'I'm very sorry. We did everything we could, but he pulled through'.

Rodney Dangerfield

When a visitor visits me in hospital, I press the button marked NURSE. That assures us of at least forty-five minutes of undisturbed privacy.

Dorothy Parker

Having a baby is like taking your lower lip and forcing it over your head.

Carol Burnett

I was born by Caesarean section, but not so you'd notice. It's just that when I leave a house, I go out through the window.

Steven Wright

His ideas of first-aid stopped short at squirting soda-water.

P.G. Wodehouse

To lose a lover or even a husband or two during the course of one's life can be vexing. But to lose one's teeth is a catastrophe.

Hugh Wheeler

They called me mad, and I called them mad, and damn them, they outvoted me.

Nathaniel Lee

She omitted to tell me she had thrush until I had actually signed her into the Great Portland Street Academy. I've put her on a crash course of natural yoghurt which rather messily has to be applied to the parts as well as swallowed, and I've sworn her to celibacy until the start of the flat racing season, which opens at Doncaster on 22 March, exactly one day after J.S. Bach's birthday.

Jeffrey Bernard

If you really want to clear your system out, sit on a piece of cheese and swallow a mouse.

Johnny Carson

I won't say Elizabeth Taylor is fat, but she had a face-lift, and there was enough skin left over to make another person.

Joan Rivers

If somebody has a bad heart, they can plug this jack in at night as they go to bed and it will monitor their heart throughout the night. And the next morning, when they wake up dead, there'll be a record.

Mark Fowler

Constipation has made me a walking time bomb.

Beryl King

Why do you need four doctors? Isn't one enough to kill anyone?

Molière

Medicine and Doctors

I joined a health club last year, spent four hundred bucks.
Haven't lost a pound. Apparently, you have to show up.

Rich Ceisler

His mind is completely gone. The wheel is still going round
but the gerbil has left the cage.

Jim Bowen

Music

 **Music**

I was not able to detect in the vocal parts of Parsifal anything that might with confidence be called rhythm or tune or melody.

Mark Twain

I believe that the kidnapping of Frank Sinatra Jr. was carried out by music critics.

Oscar Levant

Claude Debussy played the piano with the lid down.

Robert Bresson

The darting eyes of James Galway give the impression of a man permanently watching tennis at Wimbledon; his haunted expression may well be divine retribution for his appalling recording of 'Annie's Song' he made in the 1970s, a rendition that inspired a million tone-deaf kids to take up the flute.

Victor Lewis-Smith

Daughters, lock up your mothers, Daniel O'Donnell is in town.

Patrick Murray

As a sex symbol Tom Jones is nothing short of inexplicable.

Sheridan Morley

Music-hall songs provide the dull with wit, just as proverbs provide them with wisdom.

Somerset Maugham

Signor Tamberlik sings in a doubtful falsetto and his movements are unmeaning and frequently absurd. For the C sharp in the celebrated duet he substituted a strange description of shriek at about that pitch. The audience, ever appreciative of vocal curiosities, eagerly redemanded it.

George Bernard Shaw

Music makes a nation's disposition more gentle – for example 'The Marseillaise'.

Gustave Flaubert

You want something by Bach? Which one – Johann Sebastian or Jacques Offen?

Victor Borge

The most expensive solution would be to blow up all the opera houses.

Pierre Boulez

No one should be allowed to play the violin until he has mastered it.

Jim Fiebig

A guy who hangs around with musicians is called a drummer.

Lisa Fuglie

Miss Marcia Devin sang 'I Will Not Pass This Way Again', giving obvious pleasure to the entire congregation.

Leo Rosten

George Gershwin played us a medley of his hit.

Oscar Levant

The opera was pretty good. Even the music was nice.

Yogi Berra

I have witnessed and greatly enjoyed the first act of everything which Wagner created, but the effect on me has always been so powerful that one act was quite sufficient; whenever I have witnessed two acts I have gone away physically exhausted; and whenever I have ventured an entire opera the result has been the next thing to suicide.

Mark Twain

Listening to Vaughan William's Fifth Symphony is like staring at a cow for forty-five minutes.

Aaron Copland

To test the acoustics at his new Bayrueth theatre, soldiers from the local garrison were brought in to squat on the floor and Wagner was moved to describe them as the ideal audience on three counts:
1. They were all in their places before the music began.
2. They did not talk or fidget while it was being played.
3. When it was over they made no pretence of having understood anything of what they had seen or heard and so refrained from airing their opinions about it.

Robert Hartford

When something is not worth saying, sing it.

Gioacchino Rossini

If the Almighty himself played the violin, the credits would still read Rubenstein, God, and Piatigorsky, in that order.

Jascha Heifetz

It takes four jazz trumpeters to change a lightbulb. One to actually change it and the other three to discuss how Dizzy Gillespie would have done it.

Geoff Boardwell

I'd like to see a nude opera, because when they hit those high notes, I bet you can really see it in those genitals.

Jack Handey

Paul, George, and Ringo are recording a song using the last of John's unreleased tapes. It goes 'Hello, this is the Lennon residence, I can't come to the phone right now…'

Chris Cox

Now, ladies and contraltos, if you will look to your parts, you will see where the gentlemen and tenors come in.

Thomas Beecham

The best way to confuse a drummer is to put a sheet of music in front of him.

Lizzi Davenport

I couldn't warm to Chuck Berry even if I was cremated next to him.

Keith Richards

 **Music**

Jazz is a terrible revenge by the culture of the blacks on that of the whites.

Ignacy Paderewski

The Battle of Crete, like German opera, was too long and too loud.

Evelyn Waugh

Puccini wrote marvellous operas, but dreadful music.

Dmitri Shostakovich

The public doesn't want new music: the main thing it demands of a composer is that he be dead.

Arthur Honegger

Prince looks like a dwarf who's been dipped in a bucket of pubic hair.

Boy George

The whole point of entering the Eurovision Song Contest is to try to come last – a coveted position which the crafty Finns have more or less cornered for years.

Karl Shaw

In the first movement alone of Bruckner's Seventh Symphony, I took note of six pregnancies and at least four miscarriages.

Thomas Beecham

A three-voice fugue resembles a family of identical triplets in perfect agreement, or a madman talking to himself.

Ned Rorem

Never encourage the brass, except with a curt glance, in order to give an important entrance cue.

Richard Strauss

For my part, if I had the power, I would insist on all oratorios being sung in the costume of the period – with a possible exception in the case of the Creation.

Ernest Newman

I wonder what Gary Wilmot did with the money his mother gave him for singing lessons?

Victor Lewis-Smith

Her singing was mutiny on the high C's.

Hedda Hopper

Mick Jagger and I really liked each other a lot. We talked all night. We had the same views on nuclear disarmament.

Jerry Hall

I don't mind what language an opera is sung in as long as it is a language I don't understand.

Edward Appleton

 **Music**

I say Carmina and you say Burana,
I say Catulli and you say Carmina,
Carmina! Burana!
Catulli! Carmina!
Let's call the whole thing Orff.

Adrian Corston

Jazz isn't dead, it just smells funny.

Frank Zappa

I don't know anything about music. In my line of work you
don't have to.

Elvis Presley

I can't sing. As a singist I am not a success. I am saddest
when I sing. So are those who hear me. They are even
sadder than I am.

Artemus Ward

All Bach's last movements are like the running of a sewing
machine.

Arnold Bax

Mozart was happily married – but his wife wasn't.

Victor Borge

How do you know when it's time to tune your bagpipes?
E.K. Kruger

Elton John's writing is limited to songs about dead blondes.
Keith Richards

I'm worried that the person who thought up Muzak may be thinking up something else.

Lily Tomlin

The sonatas of Mozart are unique; they are too easy for children, and too difficult for artists.

Artur Schnabel

I have already heard Debussy's music. I had better not go; I will start to get accustomed to it and finally like it.

Nickolai Rimsky-Korsakov

Tina Turner is the only rock singer whose legs go all the way up to her armpits.

Kenny Everett

Elvis Costello looks like Buddy Holly after drinking a can of STP Oil Treatment.

Dave Marsh

The Anarchist's national anthem is an international anthem that consists of 365 raspberries blown in quick succession to the tune of "Camptown Races". Nobody has to stand up for it, nobody has to listen to it, and, even better, nobody has to play it.

Mike Harding

Yoko Ono's voice sounded like an eagle being goosed.

Ralph Novak

 **Music**

There are some good people in it, but the orchestra as a whole is equivalent to a gang bent on destruction.

John Cage

I love Beethoven, especially his poems.

Ringo Starr

This piano piece is to be played with both hands in the pocket.

Erik Satie

Beethoven's last quartets were written by a deaf man and should be listened to only by a deaf man.

Thomas Beecham

She helps him up, and the two dance a pas de deux, after which Leonid tries to impress her by rolling his eyes until he has to be carried to a comfort station.

Woody Allen

Nationalities and Places

The English are good at forgiving their enemies; it releases them from the obligation of liking their friends.

P.D. James

German ought to be gently and reverently set aside among the dead languages, for only the dead have time to learn it.

Mark Twain

My father was from Donegal – he didn't metabolise ethanol very well.

George Carlin

From the earliest times the Welsh have been looked upon as an unclean people. It is thus that they have preserved their racial integrity. Their sons and daughters mate freely with sheep but not with human kind, except their own blood relations.

Evelyn Waugh

The Todas of Southern India are of the opinion that if a girl is still a virgin at her wedding, her maternal uncle will be taken ill and die.

Mark Fowler

If you do somebody in Ireland a favour, you make an enemy for life.

Hugh Leonard

When in Turkey, do as the turkeys do.

Honoré De Balzac

Japanese Prime Ministers are just glorified transistor salesmen.

Charles De Gaulle

Whenever the literary German dives into a sentence, that is the last you are going to see of him till he emerges on the other side of the Atlantic with his verb in his mouth.

Mark Twain

My club is world famous – we get coaches from as far away as Sheffield.

Bernard Manning

Arrival-Angst is closely connected with guilt, with the dread of something terrible having happened during our absence. Death of parents. Entry of bailiffs. Flight of loved one. Sensations worse at arriving in the evening than in the morning, and much worse at Victoria and Waterloo, than at Paddington.

Cyril Connolly

Everybody has a right to pronounce foreign names as he chooses.

Winston Churchill

The best empire-builder is the colonist who has good reasons for not coming home again.

David Somervell

The Israelis are now what we call 'enemy-friends'.

Yasser Arafat

Since Finland first entered the Eurovision fray in 1961 they have appeared in the competition 34 times, finishing last on an unequalled nine occasions with songs which sounded as though they were originally designed to frighten elks.

Karl Shaw

The first commandment of life in Ireland would appear to be, thou shalt never under any circumstances wash a car.

Rowan Atkinson

The FA are optimistic about England's bid to stage the World Cup in twenty thousand and six.

Peter Snow

German is the most extravagantly ugly language. It sounds like someone using a sick bag on a 747.

Willy Rushton

New York now leads the world's great cities in the number of people around whom you shouldn't make a sudden move.

David Letterman

A nation is a people who share a common misconception as to their origins and a common antipathy towards their neighbours.

Eric Hobsbawm

Don't worry about the world coming to an end today. It's already tomorrow in Australia.

Charles Schultz

He was shouting in a sort of Franglais – 'I will frappez votre teeth so far down votre gorge, you'll be able to manger avec your derriere'.

Victor Lewis-Smith

The English may not be the best writers in the world; but they are incomparably the best dull writers.

Raymond Chandler

Sign in a Paris restaurant:
A ten percent discount is cheerfully given to customers who do not attempt to order in French.

Leo Rosten

Bernie Slevin was half Scottish and half Irish. Half of him wanted to get drunk while the other half didn't want to pay for it.

Jack Charlton

Traditionally, most of Australia's exports come from overseas.

Keppel Enderbery

I love Americans, but not when they try to speak French. What a blessing it is that they never try to speak English.

H.H. Munro

Blackpool is a town which looks like as if it's helping police with their enquiries.

Victor Lewis-Smith

American husbands are the best in the world; no other husbands are so generous to their wives, or can be so easily divorced.

Elinor Glyn

Holland lies so low it is saved only by being dammed.

Thomas Hood

In Russia everything is forbidden. In Germany, everything is forbidden unless it is permitted. In Britain, everything is permitted unless it is forbidden. And in Italy, everything is permitted whether it is forbidden or not.

P.J. O'Rourke

People say New Yorkers can't get along. Not true. I saw two New Yorkers, complete strangers, sharing a cab. One guy took the tyres and the radio; the other guy took the engine.

David Letterman

At first the dive-bombing was impressive, but after half an hour deadly monotonous. It was like everything German - overdone.

Evelyn Waugh

Tip the world over on its side and everything loose will land in Los Angeles.

Frank Lloyd Wright

To Americans, English manners are far more frightening than none at all.

George Mikes

The tourist in Ireland has only to ask and he will be directed to something; whether or not it is what he thinks he is looking for is another matter.

Ciarán Carson

For God's sake, madam, do not say in England that the quality of air in Ireland is good, or they will surely tax it.

Jonathan Swift

On a clear day, from the terrace, you can't see Luxembourg at all. This is because a tree is in the way.

Alan Coren

Melbourne is a ghost town. You couldn't even get a parachute to open here after 10pm.

Max Bygraves

The definition of an American virgin is any girl that can run faster than Bill Clinton.

Iain Dale

After a day smiling like insane persons and talking about how they would very much like to help handicapped animals, the Miss America contestants go back to their hotel rooms and unwind by smoking enormous cigars and spitting out the window onto elderly pedestrians.

Dave Barry

We should export all of our toxic waste to third world countries because underpopulated countries in Africa are vastly underpolluted.

Lawrence Summers

Americans have different ways of saying things. They say 'elevator', we say 'lift'; they say 'President', we say 'stupid psychopathic git'.

Alexei Sayle

The reason there is so little crime in Germany is that it's against the law.

Alex Levin

Like so many Americans, she was trying to construct a life that made sense from things she found in gift shops.

Kurt Vonnegut Jr.

I don't have a problem with parking in San Francisco. I drive a forklift.

Jim Samuels

Am I to understand that an overweight Italian singing in his own language is part of my English heritage?

Terence Dicks

Speculation is that the Swedes are slowly boring themselves to death. This is certainly the case if their cars and movies are any indication.

P.J. O'Rourke

In English history the king always turned out to be a syphilitic hunchbacked lunatic dwarf whose basic solution to virtually all problems, including humidity, was to have somebody's head cut off. Henry VIII could barely get through a day without beheading a wife.

Dave Barry

Dublin, though a place much worse than London, is not so bad as Iceland.

Samuel Johnson

Edna Everage is Australia's revenge for penal colonisation.

Michael Parkinson

Arkansas is very proud of Bill Clinton – all those women coming forward and none of them is his sister!

John Simmons

It is all very well to call Ned Kelly a white-livered cur, a bully, a coward, a liar and a psychotic murderer, but to actually name him as a queer is going too far.

Keith Dunstan

Life is very important to many Americans.

Bob Dole

In a British hotel, the words 'Can I help you sir?' mean roughly 'What the hell do you want?'

Kingsley Amis

Organised crime in America takes in forty billion dollars a year and spends very little on office supplies.

Woody Allen

No matter how many times I visit New York City, I am always struck by the same thing: a yellow taxi cab.

Scott Adams

We British must ski on.

Charles Windsor

Ireland has a great reputation as a literary nation. You walk into any pub in Dublin and it's full of writers and poets. In most other countries they're called drunks.

Ardal O'Hanlon

In the Australian Outback there are lots of men and not very many women. Out there 'Tie me kangaroo down, sport', is a love song.

Tom Pepper

He asked his brother what it was like in 'the other world', and his brother said it was not unlike Cleveland.

Woody Allen

Three failures and a fire make a Scotsman's fortune.

Alexander Hislop

The Russian Revolution simmered for years and suddenly erupted when the serfs realised that the Czar and the Tsar were the same person.

Woody Allen

In Japanese the symbol for 'crisis' is also the symbol for 'total cock-up'.

Patrick Murray

An Englishman sucked his viagra tablet instead of swallowing it. He wound up with a stiff upper lip.

Ken O'Callaghan

In Glasgow there is no such word as 'happy'. The nearest we have is 'giro' or 'blootered'!

Gregor Fisher

If all the cars in the United States were placed end to end, it would probably be Labor Day Weekend.

Doug Larson

Australia is an outdoor country. People go indoors only to use the toilet and that's a recent development.

Barry Humphries

The overall impression from the British is that they love France but would prefer if the French didn't live there.

John Mortimer

Europe – the people don't take baths and they don't speak English. No golf courses, no room service. Who needs it?

Jim McMahon

I think that's how Chicago got started. A bunch of people in New York said, 'Gee, I'm enjoying the crime and the poverty, but it just isn't cold enough. Let's go west!'

Richard Jeni

Nationalities and Places

You couldn't get me on Mars if it were the last place on earth.

Erma Cohen

Australian foreplay consists largely of the words 'Are you awake?'

Barry Humphries

Just give me your word, Mr President and I'll make the Island of Cuba into a ******* parking lot.

Alexander Haig

On the Beach is a story about the end of the world, and Melbourne sure is the right place to film it.

Neil Jillett

I am very glad to have seen the Caledonian Canal, but I don't want to see it again.

Matthew Arnold

Coming back from Canada as I crossed the border I was asked if I had any firearms, I said 'What do you need?'

Steven Wright

I am a great friend of Israel. Any country that can stand Milton Friedman as an adviser has nothing to fear from a few million Arabs.

J.K. Galbraith

The population of England is thirty million, mostly fools.

Thomas Carlyle

England is the only country in the world where the food is more dangerous than the sex.

Jackie Mason

The tragedy of Canada is that they had the opportunity to have French cuisine, British culture and American technology, and instead they ended up with British cuisine, American culture and French technology.

Will Shetterly

English is a simple, yet hard language. It consists entirely of foreign words pronounced wrongly.

Kurt Tucholsky

The Russian government's proposal to workers to pay them with bottles of vodka has been turned down. Previous proposals to pay them with toilet rolls and funeral accessories were also rejected.

Yakov Smirnoff

Inside every Australian there's an Irishman fighting an Englishman.

Phillip Royce

After illicit love and flaring drunkenness nothing appeals so much to Scotch sentiment as having been born in the gutter.

T.W. Crosland

Certain phrases stick in the throat. 'A dashing Swiss officer',
is one such.

John Russell

The German mind has a talent for making no mistakes
except the very greatest.

Clifton Fadiman

The Irish are one race of people for whom psychoanalysis is
of no use whatsoever.

Sigmund Freud

Perhaps we can at least teach the Americans that there are
better things to do with a cigar than Clinton seems to realise.

Auberon Waugh

The Swiss have an interesting army. Five hundred years
without a war. Pretty impressive. Also pretty lucky for
them. Ever see that little Swiss Army knife they have to fight
with? Not much of a weapon there. Corkscrews, bottle
openers. 'Come on buddy, let's go. You get past me, the guy
in back of me, he's got a spoon. Back off, I've got the toe
clippers right here'.

Jerry Seinfeld

The Italians should never, ever been let in on the invention
of the motor car.

Bill Bryson

The USA leads the world in exporting jobs.

Dan Quayle

It is proposed to call the new capital of Australia Myola. It sounds like the last despairing cry of an Italian prostitute.

Billy Hughes

Edinburgh is a cross between Copenhagen and Barcelona, except that in Copenhagen and Barcelona they speak more understandable English.

John Malkovich

The English think soap is civilisation.

Heinrich Von Treitschke

The Polish army has just bought ten thousand septic tanks. When they learn how to drive them they are going to invade Russia.

Larry Wilde

I moved to New York City for my health. I'm paranoid and New York is the only place where my fears are justified.

Anita Weiss

A Bavarian is half-way between an Austrian and a human being.

Otto Von Bismarck

The most striking thing about the City of Venice is the complete absence of the smell of horse dung.

Alphonse Allais

If God doesn't destroy Hollywood Boulevard, he owes Sodom and Gomorrah an apology.

Jay Leno

Russia is the only country in the world you can be homesick for while you're still in it.

John Updike

I always enjoy appearing before a British audience. Even if they don't feel like laughing they nod their heads to show they've understood.

Bob Hope

The most frightening fact about AIDS is that it can be spread by normal sex between men and women. Fortunately, this is still rare in Scotland.

Joan Burnie

It is not necessary to have relatives in Kansas City to be unhappy.

Groucho Marx

Politics

 **Politics**

Deep down I am quite conservative, so I vote Labour.

Christopher Logue

Goebbels wore lifts in his shoes yet still qualified as a midget.

Victor Lewis-Smith

I am a more virtuous man than President Kennedy or President Bush, two notorious philanderers.

Saddam Hussein

I never vote for the best candidate, I vote for the one who will do the least harm.

Franklin Dane

I disapprove of what you say and I will defend to the death my right to prevent you from saying it.

Dominic Cleary

He couldn't find his ass with both hands.

Lyndon B. Johnson

Bill Clinton should remember that goats don't talk.

Yasser Arafat

There is a winter you know in Russia. Hitler forgot about this. He must have been very loosely educated. We all hear about it at school, but he forgot it. I have never made such a bad mistake as that.

Winston Churchill

The new definition of silence: Dan Quayle and Bill Clinton telling their Vietnam war stories to each other.

Iain Dale

Montgomery was in defeat unbeatable; in victory, unbearable.

Winston Churchill

There are too many politicians who believe, with a conviction based on experience, that you can fool all of the people all of the time.

Franklin P. Adams

To an MP's wife nobody is common, provided he's on the register.

George Bernard Shaw

If I were two-faced, would I be using this one?

Abraham Lincoln

The man with the best job in the country is the Vice President. All he has to do is to get up every morning and say, 'How's the President?'

Will Rogers

Democracy becomes a government of bullies tempered by editors.

Ralph Waldo Emerson

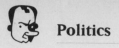

My opponents have done a full 360° turn on this issue.
Mary McAleese

What makes Clint Eastwood, a middle aged actor who has played with a chimp, think he could have a future in politics?
Ronald Reagan

Democracy is the art and science of running the circus from the monkey cage.
H.L. Mencken

Pat Buchanan is racist, homophobic, xenophobic and sexist. In a word, he's the perfect Republican candidate.
Bill Press

When Bob Dole does smile, he looks as if he's just evicted a widow.
Mike Royko

Crime does not pay – as well as politics.
Alfred E. Neumann

Dan Quayle is more stupid than Ronald Reagan put together.
Matt Groening

The House of Peers, throughout the war, did nothing in particular, and did it very well.
W.S. Gilbert

If elected, I will win.

Pat Paulsen

I've been married to one Marxist and one Fascist, and neither one would take the garbage out.

Lee Grant

It is useless to hold a person to anything he says while he's in love, drunk, or running for office.

Shirley MacLaine

Calvin Coolidge's perpetual expression was that of someone smelling something burning on a stove.

Sherwin Cook

Anyone who is capable of getting themselves elected President should on no account be allowed to do the job.

Douglas Adams

Richard Nixon inherited some good instincts from his Quaker forebears, but by diligent hard work, he overcame them.

James Reston

Calvin Coolidge didn't say much and when he did, he didn't say much.

Will Rogers

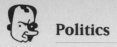

The year 1908 saw the election of the first US president to successfully weigh more than three hundred pounds, William Howard Taft, who ran on a platform of reinforced concrete and who, in a stirring inauguration speech, called for 'a bacon cheeseburger and a side order of fries'.

Dave Barry

I believe that Ronald Reagan can make this country what it once was – an Arctic region covered with ice.

Steve Martin

In those days he was wiser than he is now – he used frequently to take my advice.

Winston Churchill

A citizen of America will cross the ocean to fight for democracy, but won't cross the street to vote in a national election.

Bill Vaughan

Bill Clinton thinks international affairs means dating girls from out of town.

Tom Clancy

Nobody believes the unofficial spokesman, but everybody trusts an unidentified source.

Ron Nesen

The word 'politics' is derived from the word 'poly', meaning 'many', and the word, 'ticks', meaning 'blood-sucking parasites'.

Larry Hardiman

We hang the petty thieves and appoint the great ones to public office.

Aesop

A child can go only so far in life without potty training. It is not mere coincidence that six of the last presidents were potty trained, not to mention half of the nation's state legislators.

Dave Barry

We are ready for any unforeseen event that may or may not occur.

Dan Quayle

The House of Lords must be the only institution in the world which is kept efficient by the persistent absenteeism of most of its members.

Herbert Samuel

If you want to trace your family tree, all you have to do is to run for public office.

Patricia Vance

Watergate was worse than a crime – it was a blunder.

Richard Nixon

Politics

If ignorance ever gets to $45 a barrel, I want drilling rights on George Bush's head.

Jim Hightower

As an intellectual, Eisenhower bestowed on the games of golf and bridge all the enthusiasm and perseverance that he withheld from his books and ideas.

Emmet J. Hughes

A standing army is like a standing member. It is an excellent assurance of domestic tranquillity, but a dangerous temptation to foreign adventure.

Elbridge Gerry

If I studied all my life, I couldn't think up half the number of funny things passed in one session of congress.

Will Rogers

Death and taxes are inevitable. However, death does not get worse every time the legislators meet.

Will Rogers

A zebra cannot change its spots.

Al Gore

A revolution in politics is an abrupt change in the form of misgovernment.

Ambrose Bierce

The more you read and observe about politics, you got to admit that each party is worse than the other. The one that's out always looks the best.

Will Rogers

In our civilisation, and under our republican form of government, intelligence is so highly honoured that it is rewarded by exemption from the cares of office.

Ambrose Bierce

You look into Dan Quayle's eyes and you get the feeling someone else is driving.

David Letterman

If you're the sort of person who gets your simple pleasures out of life tearing wings off dying butterflies, then Barry Unsworth's your man.

Bill Hayden

Diplomacy is lying in state.

George Herbert

Any political party that can't cough up anything better than a trecherous brain-damaged old vulture like Hubert Humphrey deserves every beating it can get. They don't hardly make 'em like Hubert anymore – but just to be on the safe side, he should be castrated anyway.

Hunter S. Thompson

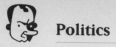# Politics

There is about as much love between Hillary and Bill Clinton as between those other two great allies Stalin and Hitler.

Taki

He is so fat he can be his own running mate.

Johnny Carson

To forcibly remove a politician from office, one has to meet a much higher standard of dishonesty.

Michael Cooney

Joseph Chamberlain was dangerous as an enemy, untrustworthy as a friend, but fatal as a colleague.

Hercules Robinson

You don't see me at Vegas or the track throwing my money around any more, I've got a government to support.

Bob Hope

This country has come to feel the same when Congress is in session as when the baby gets hold of a hammer.

Will Rogers

Most problems don't exist until a government agency is created to solve them.

Kirk Kirkpatrick

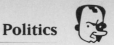

Compared to the Clintons, Reagan is living proof that a Republican with half a brain is better than a Democrat with two.

P.J. O'Rourke

Politics is not a bad profession. If you succeed there are many rewards, and if you disgrace yourself you can always write a book.

Ronald Reagan

The House of Lords is good evidence of life after death.

Baron Soper

President Clinton apparently gets so much action that every couple of weeks they have to spray WD-40 on his zipper.

David Letterman

To my mind Judas Iscariot was nothing but a low, mean, premature congressman.

Mark Twain

I will erect not only urinals but also arsenals.

Camillien Houde

I voted for the Democrats because I didn't like the way the Republicans were running the country. Which is turning out to be like shooting yourself in the head to stop your headache.

Jack Mayberry

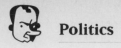

Jimmy Carter needs Billy Carter like Van Gogh needs stereo.

Johnny Carson

James Callaghan does not have much Irish blood in him. His father died when he was nine and it was his mother who brought him up.

Michael Green

If George Bush reminds many women of their first husbands, Pat Buchanan reminds women why an increasing number of them are staying single.

Judy Pearson

The Republicans have a new healthcare proposal: Just say NO to illness.

Mark Russell

Democracy means that anyone can grow up to be President, and anyone who doesn't grow up can be Vice President.

Johnny Carson

Conservatism is the political equivalent of bed-wetting.

Hywel Williams

When Lord Copper was right he said, 'Definitely, Lord Copper', when he was wrong, 'Up to a point, Lord Copper'.

Evelyn Waugh

If you put the federal government in charge of the Sahara Desert, in five years there would be a shortage of sand.

Milton Friedman

He is useless on top of the ground; he ought to be under it inspiring the cabbages.

Mark Twain

Know thyself. If you need help, call the CIA.

Mort Sahl

In Washington if you want a friend, buy a dog.

Harry Truman

I am strongly in favour of common sense, common honesty, and common decency. This makes me forever ineligible for public office.

H.L. Mencken

If life were fair, Dan Quayle would be making a living asking, "Do you want fries with that?"

John Cleese

Dan Quayle is an empty suit that goes to funerals and plays golf.

Ross Perot

 **Politics**

Choosing among Bush, Clinton and Perot was like needing clean underwear and being forced to decide between three dirty pairs.

Michael Johnson

They asked me to go in front of the Reagans. I'm not used to going in front of President Reagan, so we went out behind the Bushes.

Dan Quayle

John F. Kennedy is the enviably attractive nephew who sings an Irish ballad for the company and then winsomely disappears before the table clearing and dishwashing begin.

Lyndon B. Johnson

When your back is against the wall, the only thing to do is to turn around and fight.

John Major

Religion

✝ Religion

I'm not really a practising Jew but I keep a kosher kitchen just to spite Hitler.

Miriam Margolyes

Like a woman's dress, a sermon ought to be long enough to cover the subject but sufficiently short to arouse attention.

H. S. Taylor

Put down enthusiasm – the Church of England in a nutshell.

Mary Augusta Ward

The sacrament of confirmation in the Church of England tends to be a sort of spiritual sheep dip.

Lord Altrincham

'We need more money', said the vicar, 'for our organ repair fund – and if we can't get it by fair means, we'll have to organise another sale of work'.

J. B. Morton

It is much easier to repent of sins that we have committed that to repent of those we intend to commit.

Josh Billings

When you convert someone to an idea, you lose your faith in it.

Oscar Wilde

I read the bible – every goddamn day.

George Patton

Religion ✝

Never take a reference from a clergyman. They always want to give someone a second chance.

Lady Selborne

Forgive your enemies – if you can't get back at them any other way.

Franklin P. Jones

Dear God, you help total strangers – so why not me?

Leo Rosten

The Puritans were an extremely religious group who lived in England and did not believe in drinking or dancing or having sex with hooved animals.

Dave Barry

When I get over to the other side, I shall use my influence to have the human race drowned again, and this time drowned good, no omissions, no Ark.

Mark Twain

If there is no God, who pops up the next Kleenex?

Art Hoppe

First secure an independent income. Then practise virtue.

Aristotle

✝ Religion

There can hardly be a town in the South of England where you could throw a brick without hitting the niece of a bishop.

George Orwell

The better sort of Ishmaelites have been Christian for many centuries and will not publicly eat human flesh uncooked in Lent, without special and costly dispensation from their bishop.

Evelyn Waugh

Many people think they have religion when they merely have dyspepsia.

Robert G. Ingersoll

We must respect the other fellow's religion, but only in the sense and to the extent that we respect his theory that his wife is beautiful and his children are smart.

H.L. Mencken

I think that it can fairly be said that everything in the Holy Land is cursed.

P.J. O'Rourke

Frisbeetarianism is the belief that when you die, your soul goes up on the roof and gets stuck.

George Carlin

There is no original sin – it's all been done before.

Louis Dudek

If there is no God, who opens the doors in supermarkets?
Patrick Murray

The universe is merely a fleeting idea in God's mind – a pretty uncomfortable thought, particularly if you've just make a down payment on a house.
Woody Allen

Our dourest parsons always seemed to me to be bent on bullying God. After a few 'beseech thees' as a mere politeness, they adopted a sterner tone and told Him what they expected from Him and more than hinted He must attend to His work.
J.B. Priestley

Lead me not into temptation – I can find it for myself.
John Bernal

The only thing wrong with immortality is that it tends to go on forever.
Herb Caen

Finally, it emerged that Alan Clark, of all people, may cross the Tiber, presumably after a record-breaking session in the confessional.
Damian Thompson

The game of golf is an intensely Presbyterian activity.
Clifford Hanley

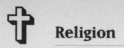

Religion

It's being proposed to surround St. Paul's with a wooden pavement: Let the Dean and Canons lay their heads together and the thing will be done.

Sydney Smith

An Act of God is defined as 'something no reasonable man could have expected'.

A. P. Herbert

Never before have I encountered such corrupt and foul-minded perversity. Have you ever considered a career in the Church?

Rowan Atkinson

The way the Catholic Church is going, we will all soon be saying the Hail Mary thus: Hiya Moll. You're the tops. You've got everything it takes, baby, and that goes for Junior too. Look Moll, you put in a word for us slobs now and when we snuff it. Amen.

Evelyn Waugh

You have to take a lighter approach now. Jumping up on a table in a busy restaurant, swinging from the ceiling fans, and screaming, 'You're all gonna burn in Hell', just scares people away.

Steven Forker

Mohammed is one of the commonest Christian names in the world.

Kid Jensen

The reason why the Irish took to Catholicism so easily was the ability of its founder to turn water into wine.

Des MacHale

I remember I was once so depressed I was going to jump out of a window on the tenth floor, so they sent a priest up to talk to me. He said 'On your mark…'.

Rodney Dangerfield

Tele-evangelists are the pro wrestlers of religion.

Steven Wright

War is just God's way of teaching us geography.

Paul Rodriguez

Saints are OK in Heaven, but they're Hell on earth.

Richard Cushing

She didn't really have any religion except for being anti-Catholic.

Randolph Stow

The first duty of a revolutionary is to get away with it.

Abbie Hoffman

History has the relation to truth that theology has to religion i.e. none to speak of.

Hal Mitchum

✝ Religion

He was a solemn, unsmiling, sanctimonious old iceberg who looked like he was waiting for a vacancy in the Trinity.

Mark Twain

Thou shalt not kill. Thou shalt not commit adultery. Don't eat pork. I'm sorry, what was that last one? Don't eat pork. God has spoken. Is that the word of God or is that pigs trying to outsmart everybody?

Jon Stewart

God is silent – now if we can only get man to shut up.

Woody Allen

I give Sammy Davis Jr. a lot of credit for becoming a Jew. I myself would not have had the courage to become a coloured person.

Dan Greenburg

What would I like the sermon to be about, vicar? I would like it to be about ten minutes.

Arthur Wellesley

The reason that God was able to create the world in seven days is that he didn't have to worry about the installed base.

Enzo Torresi

I don't know if one should pray standing, sitting, or kneeling but the finest position I ever prayed in was upside down in a well.

Saunders Guerrant

Confess your sins to the Lord and you will be forgiven;
confess them to men, and you will be laughed at.

Josh Billings

The few men who have managed to reach Heaven must be
terribly spoiled by this time.

Edgar Howe

It is easier for a camel to pass through the eye of a needle if it
is lightly greased.

Kehlog Albran

Science and Technology

Science and Technology

Time wasted only when sprinkling perfume on goat farm.
Charlie Chan

Scientists have invented something for getting chewing gum off the pavement. It is called a shoe.
Nick Percival

An intellectual is a man who doesn't know how to park a bike.
Spiro T. Agnew

We said zero, and I think any statistician will tell you that when you're dealing with very big numbers, zero must mean plus or minus a few.
William Waldegrave

Nuclear winter is the most important scientific theory since phlogiston, phrenology and Piltdown Man.
Tim Curry

Given apples and motion, the English produced Isaac Newton, the Swiss William Tell.
Malcolm Scott

My inclination to go by Air Express is confirmed by the crash they had yesterday, which will make them careful in the immediate future.
A. E. Housman

Should human beings ever step on Europa, one of Jupiter's moons, they need not fear constipation. The surface is littered with Epsom Salts, a potent laxative.

Nigel Hawkes

Error is part of the overhead of doing research.

Michael Ghiselin

Astrology proves one scientific fact, and one only; there's one born every minute.

Patrick Moore

Man is the missing link between apes and human beings.

Konrad Lorenz

Time flies like an arrow. Fruit flies like a banana. So just what are time flies, and why do they like an arrow?

Groucho Marx

They've just found a gene for shyness. They would have found it earlier but it was hiding behind a couple of other genes.

Jonathan Katz

Immediately after Orville Wright's historic 12-second flight, his luggage could not be located.

Sydney Harris

I spilled spot remover on my dog. He's gone now.

Steven Wright

Pembrook, the renegade third Wright brother, immediately set to work on the first anti-aircraft gun.

Sydney Harris

Just as you think about giving up, you see a gleam in the monitor that gives you a faint illusion of hope and satisfaction. Then you realise that it's the reflection of the hammer in your hand.

Mike Dotson

It doesn't matter if the cup is half full or half empty because whatever is in it is evaporating anyway.

Emo Philips

Scientists tell us that the fastest animal on earth, with a top speed of 120 feet per second, is a cow that has been dropped out of a helicopter.

Dave Barry

The Irish Sea is naturally radioactive, and the Sellafield discharges are less radioactive than the sea they are discharged into.

Cecil Parkinson

God is very good but He is not perfect. He made two major mistakes – mathematics, He made it too hard, and the avocado, He made the stone too big.

George Burns

Science and Technology

We inherited the planet Mars from our Yemeni ancestors three thousand years ago so we are suing NASA for trespassing.

Adam Ismail

Torture numbers, and they'll confess anything.

Gregg Easterbrook

Interestingly, according to modern astronomers, space is finite. This is a very comforting thought - particularly for people who can never remember where they have left things.

Woody Allen

Save the whales. Collect the whole set.

Steven Wright

Computers are not intelligent – they only think they are.

Steven Wright

The goal of computer science is to build something that will last until you've finished building it.

Douglas Adams

A distributed system is one in which the failure of a computer you didn't know even existed can render your own computer unusable.

Leslie Lamport

Sure, chlordane is going to kill a lot of people, but they may be dying of something else anyway.

Othal Brand

Eve and the apple was the first great step in experimental science.

James Bridie

I guess I'm just an old mad scientist at bottom. Give me an underground laboratory, half a dozen atom-smashers, and a beautiful girl in a diaphanous veil waiting to be turned into a chimpanzee, and I care not who writes the nation's laws.

S.J. Perelman

If A = B and B = C, then A = C, except where void or prohibited by law.

Roy Santoro

I don't find any correlation between age and greatness.

Woody Allen

I got a bit of moon rock once. When I broke it open it had MOON written all through it.

Ken Dodd

If computers get too powerful, we can organise them into a committee. That will do them in.

John Bradley

Science and Technology

The Universe is simply one of those things which happen
from time to time.

Edward Tyron

Irrigation of the land with seawater desalinated by nuclear
fusion power is a reality. It's called rain.

Michael McClary

The IQ of the group is the lowest IQ of a member of the
group divided by the number of people in the group.

John Coulton

I'm not afraid of flying. I'm afraid of crashing.

Neil Simon

The Universe is a big place, perhaps the biggest.

Kilgore Trout

Every body continues in its state of rest or uniform motion,
except insofar as it doesn't.

Arthur Eddington

After Lavoisier discovered oxygen, his whole family would
breathe it regularly as a show of support.

Sydney Harris

Last night I fell asleep in a satellite dish. My dreams were
broadcast all over the world.

Steven Wright

I have not lost my mind – it's backed up on disk somewhere.

Steven Wright

When I call for statistics about the rate of infant mortality,
what I want is proof that fewer babies died when I was
Prime Minister than when anyone else was Prime Minister.
That is a political statistic.

Winston Churchill

Software suppliers are trying to make their software packages
more user-friendly. Their best approach, so far, has been to
take all the old brochures, and stamp the words, 'user-
friendly' on the cover.

Bill Gates

Somebody ought to cross ball point pens with coat hangers
so that the pens will multiply instead of disappearing.

Steven Wright

I mix water myself. Two parts H, one part O. I don't trust
anybody.

Steven Wright

Endless loop: n. see Loop, endless.
Loop, Endless: n. see Endless loop.

Isaac Asimov

Instead of importing six Venetian gondolas for the lake in the
public gardens, why not import just a pair and let Nature
take its course?

John Kerr

Hey diddle diddle, the cat and the fiddle, but the cow has failed on its first attempt at the moon landing. That's one small step for a cow, one giant leap for the beef industry.

Flacco

Birthdays are good for you. Statistics show that people who have the most birthdays live the longest.

Larry Lorenzoni

A vacuum is a hell of a lot better than some of the stuff that Nature replaces it with.

Tennessee Williams

His theory isn't right. It isn't even wrong.

Wolfgang Pauli

If toast always lands butter-side down, and cats always land on their feet, what happens if you strap toast on the back of a cat and drop it?

Steven Wright

My husband Nick Arnstein couldn't mastermind an electric bulb into a socket.

Fanny Brice

Artificial Intelligence is no match for natural stupidity.

Wes Smith

The best car safety device is a rear-view mirror with a cop in it.

Dudley Moore

After an access cover has been secured by sixteen hold-down screws, it will be discovered that the gasket has been omitted. After the last of the sixteen mounting screws has been removed from an access cover, it will be discovered that the wrong access cover has been removed.

Della Lastra

We've got to pause and ask ourselves – just how much clean air do we need?

Lee Iacocca

Plato having defined man to be a two-legged animal without feathers, I plucked a duck and brought it into the Academy and said, 'This is Plato's man'. On which account this addition was made, to the definition – 'With broad flat nails'.

Diogenes Laertius

The Big Bang theory – in the beginning, there was nothing, which exploded.

John Irwin

A hammer was originally employed as a weapon of war, but nowadays it is used as a kind of divining rod to locate expensive car parts not far from the object we are trying to hit.

Peter Egan

Artificial intelligence is the study of how to make real computers act like the ones in movies.

Russell Baker

A scientist's wife had identical twins. He had one baptised and kept the other as a control.

Steven Wright

I worked in a pet store and people kept asking how big I'd get.

Rodney Dangerfield

I lived in a house that ran on static electricity. If you wanted to run the blender, you had to rub balloons on your head. If you wanted to cook, you had to pull off a sweater real quick.

Steven Wright

Standard mathematics has recently been rendered obsolete by the discovery that for years we have been writing the numeral five backwards.

Woody Allen

A mathematician is just a device for converting coffee into theorems.

Paul Erdös

You haven't seen untidyness until you've seen my room where gravity has failed twice in different directions.

Michael Smith

Science and Technology

The old design of a lavatory bowl with a steep inside enabled a reasonably careful gentleman to urinate without spilling a drop. The newish one makes it impossible not to bounce a couple on the floor.

Kingsley Amis

How can I tell when I have run out of invisible ink?

Steven Wright

I ran into Isosceles. He has a wonderful idea for a new triangle.

Woody Allen

O.K. so what's the speed of dark?

Steven Wright

Hardly a pure science, history is closer to animal husbandry than it is to mathematics, in that it involves selective breeding. The principal difference between the husbandryman and the historian is that the former breeds sheep or cows and the latter breeds (assumed) facts. The husbandryman uses his skills to enrich the future; the historian uses his to enrich the past. Both are usually up to their ankles in bullshit.

Tim Robbins

My fellow dinosaurs, the picture is pretty bleak. The world's climates are changing, the mammals are taking over, and we all have a brain the size of a walnut.

Gary Larson

Science and Technology

WARNING: Sending me junk e-mail will be interpreted as granting permission to bomb your offices and machine-gun your children.

Simon Slavin

Students are taught advanced concepts of Boolean Algebra, and formerly unsolvable equations are dealt with by threats of reprisals.

Woody Allen

Who is General Failure and why is he reading my hard disk?

Steven Wright

I like to torture my plants by watering them with ice cubes.

Steven Wright

The Mafia killed Einstein because he knew too much.

Steven Wright

I had to stop driving my car for a while. The tyres got dizzy.

Steven Wright

Edison's greatest achievement came in 1879 when he invented the electric company. His design was a brilliant adaptation of the simple electrical circuit: the electric company sends electricity through a wire to a customer, then immediately gets the electricity back through another wire, then (this is the brilliant part) sends it right back to the customer again.

Dave Barry

For sale parachute. Never opened. Used only once, small stain.

Steven Wright

Matter cannot be created or destroyed, nor can it be returned without a receipt.

Woody Allen

Man is the best computer we can put aboard a spacecraft and the only one that can be mass produced with unskilled labour.

Wernher von Braun

I put contact lenses in my dog's eyes. They had little pictures of cats on them. Then I took one out and he ran around in circles.

Steven Wright

The three most dangerous things in the world are a programmer with a soldering iron, a hardware type with a program patch and a user with an idea.

Rick Cook

The art of flying is to throw yourself on the ground and miss.

Douglas Adams

Diamonds are the hardest thing in the world – to give back.

Zsa Zsa Gabor

Science and Technology

The most likely way for the world to be destroyed, most experts agree, is by accident. That's where we come in; we're computer professionals. We cause accidents.

Nat Borenstein

For God's sake please read this owner's manual carefully before you unpack the device. You already unpacked it, didn't you? You unpacked it and plugged it in and turned it on and fiddled with the knobs, and now you're just starting to read the instructions, right?? We might just as well break these devices right at the factory before we ship them out.

Dave Barry

I wish I had a Kryptonite cross, because then I could keep both Dracula and Superman away.

Jack Handey

I've just bought a new microwave television set. I can watch Sixty Minutes in just twelve seconds.

Steven Wright

Social Behaviour and Manners

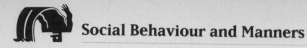

I have never liked working. To me a job is an invasion of privacy.

Danny McGoorty

Annie never changes. In fact she never even changes her clothes.

Flann O'Brien

Dear boy, it isn't that your manners are bad – it's simply that you have no manners at all.

Margot Asquith

You can never rival a millionaire if he has even the faintest inclination towards smartness. His valet wears his suits for the first three days so that they never look new, and confiscates them after three months so that they never look old.

Evelyn Waugh

A good listener is not someone who has nothing to say. A good listener is a good talker with a sore throat.

Katharine Whitehorn

There are just two classes in good society in England. The equestrian classes and the neurotic classes.

George Bernard Shaw

The dinner party was so dull that if I hadn't been there myself, I should have been bored to death.

Alexandre Dumas

My sartorial appearance was that of an unmade bed.

Dylan Thomas

Mass murderers are simply people who have had enough.

Quentin Crisp

The louder he talked of his honour, the faster we counted our spoons.

Ralph Waldo Emerson

Tact is the art of making guests feel at home when that's really where you wish they were.

George Bergman

Courtesy is opening a door for a woman you would not wish to open a bedroom door for.

Thomas Kyne

To be natural is such a very difficult pose to keep up.

Oscar Wilde

They say you shouldn't say anything about the dead unless it's good. He's dead. Good.

Moms Mabley

Actually, there is no way of making vomiting courteous. You have to do the next best thing, which is to vomit in such a way that the story you tell about it later will be amusing.

P.J. O'Rourke

I am, sir, your humble and obedient servant, which you
know, and I know, is a damn lie.

Duke of Wellington

I don't at all like knowing what people say of me behind my
back. It makes me far too conceited.

Oscar Wilde

A lady is someone who wants to punch another person in
the mouth, but doesn't.

Judith Martin

A bore is someone who persists in holding his own views
after we have enlightened him with ours.

Malcolm S. Forbes

I believe I have no prejudices whatsoever. All I need to
know is that a man is a member of the human race. That's
bad enough for me.

Mark Twain

I thoroughly disapprove of duels. If a man should challenge
me, I would take him kindly and forgivingly by the hand and
lead him to a quiet place and kill him.

Mark Twain

It was impossible to get a conversation going because
everyone was talking too much.

Yogi Berra

Class consciousness, particularly in England, has been so much inflamed that to mention a nobleman is like mentioning a prostitute sixty years ago. The new prudes say, 'No doubt such people do exist but we would sooner not hear about them.'

Evelyn Waugh

I am not eccentric. It's just that I am more alive than most people. I am an unpopular electric eel set in a pond of goldfish.

Edith Sitwell

Nobody can be exactly like me. Even I have trouble doing it.

Tallulah Bankhead

Always acknowledge a fault frankly. This will throw those in authority off their guard and give you opportunity to commit more.

Mark Twain

It is a terrible thing for a man to find out suddenly that all his life he has been speaking nothing but the truth.

Oscar Wilde

Sainthood is when you can listen to someone's tale of woe and not respond with a description of your own.

Andrew Mason

There's no pleasing some people. The trick is to stop trying.

Joel Rosenberg

'There's been an accident!' they said,
'Your servant's cut in half; he's dead!'
'Indeed!' said Mr Jones, 'and please,
Send me the half that's got the keys'.

Harry Graham

W.H. Auden always got on well with Mrs Carritt, even
though at breakfast on the first morning, he tasted his tea
and then said flatly, 'Mrs Carritt, this tea tastes like tepid piss'.

Charles Osborne

The social habits of famous people are like the sexual
practices of porcupines, which urinate on each other to
soften the quills.

P.J. O'Rourke

As I grow older I find I don't have to avoid temptation any
longer – now temptation avoids me.

Henny Youngman

A gentleman is one who never strikes a lady without
provocation.

H.L. Mencken

If you wish to appear agreeable in society you must consent
to be taught many things which you know already.

Johann Lavater

The only way to amuse some people is to slip and fall on an icy pavement.

Edgar Howe

A hat should be taken off when you greet a lady and left off for the rest of your life. Nothing looks more stupid than a hat.

P.J. O'Rourke

I must ask anyone entering the house never to contradict me in any way, as it interferes with the functioning of my gastric juices and prevents my sleeping at night.

George Sitwell

Sex is like money – very nice to have but vulgar to talk about.

Tonia Berg

Some folks can look so busy doing nothing that they seem indispensable.

Kin Hubbard

If anyone disagrees with anything I say I am quite prepared to not only retract but to deny under oath I ever said it.

Tom Lehrer

For every fellow looking for work, there are nine hiding from it.

Kin Hubbard

Reputation is character minus what you've been caught doing.

Michael Iapoce

The surest way to lose a friend is to tell him something for his own good.

Sid Ascher

My sister has a social conscience now. She still wears her fur coat, but across the back she's embroidered a notice saying 'Rest in Peace'.

Julia Willis

To get into the best society nowadays, one has either to feed people, amuse people, or shock people.

Oscar Wilde

It is difficult to say who does you the most mischief: enemies with the worst intentions or friends with the best intentions.

Edward Bulwer-Lytton

No joints on the table unless they are to be eaten.

John Morgan

He's the kind of guy who lights up a room just by flicking a switch.

Steven Wright

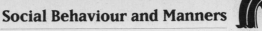

Don't look now, but there's one too many in this room and I think it's you.

Groucho Marx

Insincerity is merely a method whereby we can multiply our personalities.

Oscar Wilde

OOAQICI82QB4IP.

Audrey Austin

We read that we ought to forgive our enemies; but we do not read that we ought to forgive our friends.

Francis Bacon

There are certain tribes in Borneo that do not have a word for 'no' in their language and consequently turn down requests by nodding their heads and saying, 'I'll get back to you'.

Woody Allen

If you cannot laugh at the walking dead, who can you laugh at?

Dan Fielding

Keep a stiff upper chin.

Samuel Goldwyn

I took a course in speed-waiting. Now I can wait an hour in only ten minutes.

Steven Wright

Of course I can keep secrets. It's the people I tell them to that can't keep them.

Anthony Haden-Guest

A bachelor flat is where all the house plants are dead, but there's something growing in the refrigerator.

Marshall Williams

Don't point that beard at me, it might go off.

Groucho Marx

Never tell the truth to people that are not worthy of it.

Mark Twain

I can sympathise with everything, except suffering.

Oscar Wilde

I have a great deal of company in the house, especially in the morning when nobody calls.

Henry D. Thoreau

People who are hard, grasping and always ready to take advantage of their neighbours, become very rich.

George Bernard Shaw

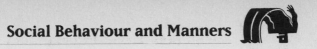

Think how many blameless lives are brightened by the blazing indiscretions of other people.

H.H. Munro

We seem to have a compulsion these days to bury time capsules in order to give people living in the future some idea of what we are like. I have prepared one of my own. I have placed in it some rather large samples of dynamite, gunpowder and nitroglycerin. My time capsule is set to go off in the year 3000. It will show them what we are really like.

Alfred Hitchcock

My grandmother took a bath every year, whether she needed it or not.

Brendan Behan

The chief excitement in a woman's life is spotting women who are fatter than she is.

Helen Rowland

Avoid the rush – get scared right away.

Joel Rosenberg

If they ever give you lined paper, write the other way.

e.e. cummings

If you ever become a mother, can I have one of the puppies?

Charles Pierce

Sport

In Rugby you kick the ball; in Soccer you kick the man if you cannot kick the ball; and in Gaelic Football you kick the ball if you cannot kick the man.

J.J. MacCarthy

You aren't out of it until you're out of it.

Yogi Berra

To be an Olympic champion, first choose your parents carefully.

Per-Olaf Astrand

Offside, the referee suggests.

Bill McLaren

Mother always told me my day was coming, but I never realised I'd end up being the shortest knight of the year.

Gordon Richards

I'm only a prawn in this game.

Brian London

The Liverpool theme song is 'You'll Never Walk Alone' – the Wimbledon theme song is 'You'll Never Walk Again'.

Tommy Docherty

I considered filing a missing persons report on Leighton James in the second half.

Bobby Gould

Sport

I can see the carrot at the end of the tunnel.

Stuart Pearce

The only sport totally without style is football. It is for many reasons an unsatisfactory game. There is something faintly idiotic about a sport the rules of which forbid a player to use his hands which are the most adaptable and efficient parts of the human body.

Quentin Crisp

I find that if you keep throwing bogeys and double bogeys at your opponents, sooner or later they will crack from the sheer pressure.

Ring Lardner

I made a two-fingered gesture towards the fans to show that I had scored twice. It must have been misinterpreted.

Paul Peschisolido

On the golf course nobody really cares what happens to you except you and your caddy. And if he's bet against you, he doesn't care either.

Lee Trevino

I became a great runner because if you're a kid in Leeds and your name is Sebastian you've got to become a great runner.

Sebastian Coe

When Ilie Nastase plays John McEnroe, it's the only time the crowd call for silence.

Jerry Girard

Always tell the truth. You may make a hole in one when you're alone on the golf course some day.

Franklin P. Jones

Ally McCoist is like dog shit in the penalty box. You don't know he's there until the damage is done.

John Hughes

It isn't over until it's over.

Yogi Berra

For the Brazilian team in the World Cup there is only one rule: Do not change girlfriends on a Monday night.

Joao Saldanha

Why they call a fellow who keeps losing all the time a good sport beats me.

Kin Hubbard

Not only is he ambidextrous but he can throw the ball with either hand.

Duffy Daugherty

And now, as the evening wears on, the shadows cast by the floodlights get longer.

David Coleman

You can tell when Kirk Stevens is thinking. When he is not thinking, he looks like an Easter Island statue with a sinus problem. When he is thinking, he still looks like that, but licks his lips.

Clive James

We need the players, because without the players we wouldn't have a team.

Howard Wilkinson

The doctors X-rayed my head and found nothing.

Dizzy Dean

I never did say that you can't be a nice guy and win. I said that if I was playing third base and my mother rounded third with a winning run I'd trip her up.

Leo Durocker

Accrington Stanley's legendary centre forward had to be turned round by his colleagues at half-time and pointed towards the opponents' goal.

Victor Lewis-Smith

I wanted to be an Olympic swimmer, but I had some problems with buoyancy.

Woody Allen

The spirit at Sheffield United is the worst I've ever known, and the tea's not much better either.

Dave Bassett

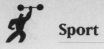

Where there's smoke there's usually a lot more smoke.

George Foreman

If a man watches three football games in a row, he should be declared legally dead.

Erma Bombeck

In a match, even when you're dead, you must never allow yourself to lie down and be buried.

Gordon Lee

Billiards is very similar to snooker, except there are only three balls and no one watches it.

Steve Davis

It's just a job. Grass grows, birds fly, waves pound the sand. I just beat people up.

Mohammed Ali

I joined as an apprentice at £25 a week. That's a bit like Ravanelli but without the noughts.

Jamie Hewitt

John McCririck looks like Worzel Gummidge after an incident with a letter bomb.

Victor Lewis-Smith

Watching Manchester City is probably the best laxative you can take.

Phil Neal

That has capped a superb season. It was an emotional night and I have one small complaint: both of the streakers were men.

Colin Todd

Golf may be played on a Sunday, not being a game within the view of the law, but being a form of moral effort.

Stephen Leacock

The only way to beat Martina Navratilova is to run over her foot in the car park.

Pam Shriver

The meek will inherit the earth, but they won't make the green in two.

Lee Trevino

Monday, in Christian countries, is the day after the baseball game.

Ambrose Bierce

My toughest fight was with my first wife.

Mohammad Ali

I got some girl's pants through the post the other day, but I didn't like them; well, they didn't fit, to be honest.

Jamie Redknapp

I don't have any prematch superstitions or habits, but I always have my packet of chocolate buttons.

Peter Beardsley

 **Sport**

Joe Bugner is a boxer with the body of a Greek sculpture but fewer moves.

Vin Shanley

Although golf was originally restricted to wealthy, overweight Protestants, today it is open to anybody who owns hideous clothing.

Dave Barry

My doctor told me I should have a complete break from football so I became manager of Wolves. The first thing I did was to open the trophy cabinet. Two Japanese prisoners of war came out.

Tommy Docherty

Patrick Tambay's hopes, which were nil before, are absolutely zero now.

Murray Walker

Nobody in the game of football should be called a genius. A genius is somebody like Norman Einstein.

Joe Theisman

I always have chicken and baked beans before a match. Chicken is the best things for quick digestion and the beans help to keep it moist – it's nothing with trying to get an extra five-yard acceleration.

Jim McIntyre

I believe that every human being has a finite allocation of heartbeats. I don't intend to waste any of mine running around doing exercises.

Neil Armstrong

Signals ambiguity should be avoided. A word sign beginning with the letter 'P' was the signal for the forwards to go right. When predictably Gareth Edwards called 'psychology', half the forwards went left.

Carwyn James

There is no use in walking five miles to fish when you can depend on being just as unsuccessful near home.

Mark Twain

Men, I want you thinking of just one word all season. One word and one word only – Super Bowl.

Bill Peterson

Running is an unnatural act, except from enemies and to the bathroom.

Robert Benchley

Gazza is a fantastic player when he isn't drunk.

Brian Laudrup

I have just named the team I would like to represent Wales in the next World Cup – Brazil.

Bobby Gould

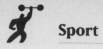 **Sport**

The referee bent over me and asked me if I knew where I was. I told him, 'You're damn right I know where I am – I'm in Madison Square Gardens getting beaten up'.
Willie Pastrano

Weight-lifting apparatus is a curious phenomenon – machines invented to replicate the back-breaking manual labour the industrial revolution relieved us of.
Sue Grafton

Up to five goals is journalism; after that, it becomes statistics.
Emmanuel Gambardella

Diamonds are forever, but oranges are for half-time.
Flacco

In weight-lifting, I don't think you should be disqualified for sudden, uncontrolled urination.
Jack Handey

For some, fishing will always be a tranquil activity for a lazy afternoon that unites sport and internal philosophising. You have a box of maggots at one hand and a plate of sandwiches at the other, and your only worry is if you mix up the two.
Peter Watts

Congratulations to Johnny Bench on breaking my record. I always thought the record would stand until it was broken.
Yogi Berra

We have nothing to do with the England men's cricket team. Some of them are quite nice people, even though they don't win as often as we do.

Rachel Hayhoe-Flint

Horse sense is the thing a horse has which keeps it from betting on people.

W.C. Fields

The ideal board of directors should be made up of three men – two dead and the other dying.

Tommy Docherty

Fishing is a delusion entirely surrounded by liars in old clothes.

Don Marquis

Here's a reason to smile: every seven minutes of every day, someone in an aerobics class pulls a hamstring.

Robin Williams

Hi. I'm here to pick up the Pope's Superbowl tickets.

Ben Salmon

The voice of the rugby commentator Winston McCarthy was like the love call of two pieces of sandpaper.

Tony O'Reilly

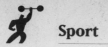

It is difficult to play attractive football at England–Scotland games when the chant is 'Gie us an English heid!'

Lou Macari

The hallmark of a great cricket captain is the ability to win the toss at the right time.

Richie Benaud

I'm a scratch golfer. I write down all my good scores and scratch out all my bad ones.

Charles Schultz

I will not permit thirty men to travel four hundred miles to agitate a bag of wind.

Andrew White

There will be more football in a moment, but first we've got the highlights of the Scottish League Cup Final.

Gary Newbon

I can talk a lot on any subject – as long as it's football.

Tommy Docherty

My wife made me join a bridge club. I jump off next Tuesday.

Rodney Dangerfield

We don't need referees in basketball, but it gives the white guys something to do.

Charles Barkley

Gentlemen, it is better to have died a small boy than to
fumble this football.

John Heisman

There are so few women snooker players because they've got
big breasts that can get in the way of the cue action.

Jimmy White

The Oxford rowing crew — eight minds with but a single
thought, if that.

Max Beerbohm

Personally, I have always looked upon cricket as merely
organised loafing.

William Temple

Any time Detroit scores more than a hundred points and
holds the other team below a hundred points, they almost
always win.

Doug Collins

Manchester United sacked me as nicely as they could. It was
one of the nicest sackings I've had.

Tommy Docherty

Theatre and Criticism

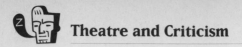

The Roly–Poly dancers on my show were built in the days when meat was cheap.

Les Dawson

One hypothesis claims that there are only seven jokes – in which case Hale and Pace have not yet heard six of them.

Victor Lewis-Smith

Men go to the theatre to forget; women, to remember.

George Nathan

I observe just one old showbusiness tradition – never fart in a dressing-room without windows.

Norman Caley

The theatre was so empty night after night, monks started using it as a short cut to vespers.

Les Dawson

Bernard Manning is a generous man – he'd give you the tent off his back.

Jimmy Tarbuck

Nuns sing in cloisters. Miss Andrews (who plays Maria) sings in her bedroom. Christopher Plummer sings in self-defense.

Philip Oakes

The play *Halfway to Hell* grossly underestimates the distance.

Brooks Atkinson

A hand-picked cast will bring my childhood to life. They will tastefully re-enact my wedding night and Norm's first urological accident.

Edna Everage

I've never much enjoyed going to plays. The unreality of painted people standing on a platform saying things they've said to each other for months is more than I can overlook.

John Updike

The first qualification for a dramatic critic is the capacity to sleep while sitting bolt upright.

William Archer

A pizza with breasts, Weisz walked through the part as if she had cotton wool in her ears and had refused to read the rest of the script on the grounds that she wanted to keep lunch down.

A.A. Gill

The first time I saw The Goons, it suddenly struck me that comedy needn't be funny.

Alexei Sayle

Dean Martin's acting is so poor that even his impersonation of a drunk is unconvincing.

Harry Medved

The only time my friends laughed at me was when I told them I was going to become a comedian.

Robin Greenspan

The people on the stage were making such a racket I could hardly hear what the audience were saying.

Henry Parker

Don't clap too hard – it's a very old building.

John Osborne

There are only two kinds of director in the theatre. Those who think they are God and those who are sure of it.

Rhetta Hughes

Alexander Woollcott looked like something that had gotten loose from Macy's Thanksgiving Day Parade.

Harpo Marx

There is something about a long queue at the box office that brings a lump to my wallet.

Eli Wallach

Alexei Sayle is about as funny as an outbreak of rabies in a guide dog's home.

Bernard Manning

Theatre and Criticism

Oh, Calcutta! is the sort of show that gives pornography a bad name.

Clive Barnes

The worst actress in the company is always the manager's wife.

H.L. Mencken

In the first scene Ruth Gordon is on the left side of the stage and the audience has to imagine that she is eating dinner in a crowded restaurant. In scene two she runs over to the right side of the stage and the audience has to imagine she is in her own drawing room. And the second night she has to imagine that there is an audience out front.

George S. Kaufman

I remember coming across George Bernard Shaw at the Grand Canyon and finding him peevish and refusing to admire it or even look at it properly. He was jealous of it.

J.B. Priestley

Hale and Pace are the world's only double act consisting of two straight men.

Victor Lewis-Smith

Ladies, just a little more virginity, if you don't mind.

Herbert Beerbohm Tree

Theatre and Criticism

The theatre has been designed for some vanished race of dwarves with bat ears and hawk eyes. The original audience could see round pillars, catch a mumbled aside bounced off the prompter, and divine which of the three blurred pink young men in identical sports jackets is actually moving his lips at any moment.

Alan Brien

Jimmy Tarbuck doesn't tell gags – he just refreshes your memory.

Bernard Manning

Just before the curtain went up, we saw the technicians making last minute alterations to the audience's chairs. Just as well because there was obviously something wrong with them. They were facing the stage.

Victor Lewis-Smith

What is this, an audience or an oil painting?

Milton Berle

When Mrs Patrick Campbell is good, she's divinely good; but when she's bad – oh, my God!

Herbert Beerbohm Tree

If one wants to see people naked one doesn't go to the theatre, one goes to a Turkish bath.

Noel Coward

Gary Cooper acquired a reputation as a great actor by just thinking hard about the next line.

King Vidor

Shaw writes his plays for the ages – the ages between five and twelve.

George Nathan

Edith Sitwell is genuinely bogus.

Christopher Hassall

One of the many neglected musicals favoured by Mr Marshall Fisher features a singing, tap dancing Gandhi on hunger strike.

Dalya Alberge

Working with Glenda Jackson was like being run over by a Bedford truck.

Oliver Reed

John Cleese emits an air of overwhelming vanity combined with some unspecific nastiness, like a black widow spider in heat. But nobody seems to notice. He could be reciting 'Fox's Book of Martyrs' in Finnish and these people would be rolling out of their seats.

Roger Gellert

Derek Jacobi will always be a fine actor but he will never be a great actor until he is circumcised.

Noel Coward

I was once offered a part in Romeo and Juliet. They weren't worried about my acting but they thought I would look sensational leaning over a balcony.

Dolly Parton

Olivier is a tour de force. Wolfit is forced to tour.

Hermione Gingold

A deep and fundamental loathing of every syllable and nuance of Bob Monkhouse is one of the cornerstones of my critical edifice.

A.A. Gill

The two men met in London at rehearsals for *Murder in the Cathedral* (at that time entitled *Million Dollar Legs*).

Woody Allen

When somebody once addressed Edith Evans as 'Ma' she turned to the bystanders and said 'I do not recall giving birth to that man'.

Michael Green

Alec Guinness wore a blond hairpiece which was too bright and remained blandly intact even after he had been beaten up and buggered by twelve Turks.

Noel Coward

You won't find anything wrong with Jack Lemmon. But if you do, for heaven's sake let the rest of us know.

Sidney Poitier

Lovborg's work can be divided into three periods. First came the series of plays dealing with anguish, despair, dread, fear, and loneliness (the comedies).

Woody Allen

Never work with children, animals or Denholm Elliot.

Gabriel Byrne

I cannot say that Mailer was drunk the whole time he was on camera. I can only hope he was drunk.

Stanley Kaufman

Robert Redford has turned almost alarmingly blond – he's gone past platinum, he must be plutonium; his hair is coordinated with his teeth.

Pauline Kael

Raquel Welch's major talent was her ability to stand up on stage without toppling over.

Marvin Kitman

W.E. Henley has fought a good fight and has had to face every difficulty except popularity.

Oscar Wilde

On stage, speak clearly, don't bump into people, and if you must have motivation think of your pay packet on Friday.

Philip Hoare

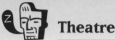

The actor and the streetwalker; the two oldest professions in the world – ruined by amateurs.

Alexander Woollcott

Dennis Potter was Dylan Thomas and Bernard Levin out for a night at a strip club.

Peter Preston

Show business is like sex. When it's wonderful, it's wonderful. But when it isn't very good, it's still all right.

Max Wall

Paul Newman delivered his lines with the emotional fervour of a conductor announcing local stops.

James Cameron

Miscellaneous

# Miscellaneous

Thanks to the interstate highway system, it is now possible to travel across the country from coast to coast without seeing anything.

Charles Kuralt

Those who built fortifications, moats and defences around castles seem to have had a blind spot about every castle's really vulnerable point – the gift shop. All a determined enemy had to do was to overpower the two old ladies who work there and the whole castle was soon taken.

Bill Bailey

I would like to die from hypothermia brought about by the breeze from my slave girls' ostrich feather fans.

Daire O'Brien

Though extremely fat when he appears in public, in private life Mr Chesterton is in fact quite slim.

Stephen Leacock

Celebrities have an obligation to have a cause to live for – I chose gay rights. I joined it and worked for it and then I quit; why? Because that organisation is infiltrated with homosexuals.

Steve Martin

I don't understand the police – how can they expect me to show them my driving licence when they took it away last year?

Gracie Allen

The proper office of a friend is to side with you when you are in the wrong. Nearly anybody will side with you when you are in the right.

Mark Twain

In 1802 every hereditary monarch was insane.

Walter Bagehot

You can cover it up, but you can never quite forget it, as the woman said as she pulled the hat down over her son's third eye.

Heinrich Hoffmann

Two women shouting at each other across the street from their top windows can never agree, because they are arguing from different premises.

Sydney Smith

Work is the greatest thing in the world, so we should always save some of it for tomorrow.

Don Herold

If you don't miss a few planes every year you are spending too much time at airports.

Paul Martin

This agoraphobic skinhead said to me 'OK, in'.

Alexei Sayle

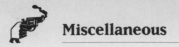

So many pedestrians, so little time.

Robin Williams

There is nothing in the world I wouldn't do for Bob Hope and there is nothing he wouldn't do for me. And that's the way we spend our lives, doing nothing for each other.

Bing Crosby

Tom Seaver asked me what time it was, I said 'You mean now?'

Yogi Berra

Mail your packages early so the post office can lose them in time for Christmas.

Johnny Carson

I'd cross an Alp to see a village idiot of quality.

Norman Douglas

Everything comes to him who waits, except a loaned book.

Kin Hubbard

A friend of mine, Joe Parts, joined the army. He was immediately promoted to corporal.

Andy Collins

No admittance. Not even to authorised personnel.

Douglas Adams

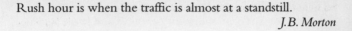

Rush hour is when the traffic is almost at a standstill.

J.B. Morton

I might give up my life for my friend, but he had better not ask me to do up a parcel.

Logan Smith

I make jail so unpleasant that they won't even think about doing something that could bring them back.

Joe Arpaio

If aliens land in Washington, and park illegally, we will definitely give them tickets.

Kenny Bryson

It is no coincidence that in no known language does the phrase "As pretty as an airport" appear.

Douglas Adams

Moses dragged us for forty years through the desert to bring us to the one place in the Middle East where there was no oil.

Golda Meir

Infamy, infamy, they've all go it in for me.

Kenneth Williams

Excess on occasion is exhilarating. It prevents moderation from acquiring the deadening effect of a habit.

Somerset Maugham

 **Miscellaneous**

If there was a little room somewhere in the British Museum that contained only about twenty exhibits and good lighting, easy chairs, and a notice imploring you to smoke, I believe I should become a museum man.

J.B. Priestley

I checked into a hotel and they had towels from my house.

Mark Guido

Gunner Octavian Neat would suddenly appear naked in a barrack room and say, 'Does anybody know a good tailor?' or 'Gentlemen – I thinks there's a thief in the battery'.

Spike Milligan

Nature played a cruel trick on her by giving her a waxed moustache.

Alan Bennett

A lie is a very poor substitute for the truth, but the only one discovered to date.

Mark Twain

The only solution to the violence problem is to take all the violent people out and shoot them.

Emo Philips

You know it's not a good wax museum if there are wicks coming out of people's heads.

Rick Reynolds

I never put on a pair of shoes until I've worn them for a few months.

Samuel Goldwyn

People are more violently opposed to fur than leather because it's safer to harass rich women then motorcycle gangs.

Alexei Sayle

I'm not concerned with all hell breaking loose, but that a part of hell will break loose. That would be much harder to detect.

George Carlin

Why does the Air Force need expensive new bombers? Have the people we've been bombing over the years been complaining?

George Wallace

For a while I didn't have a car – I had a helicopter. I had no place to park it, so I just tied it to a lamp post and left it running.

Steven Wright

No matter where you go, there you are.

Bob Topping

Let's have some new cliches.

Samuel Goldwyn

Human beings who are unique in having the ability to learn from the experience of others, are also remarkable for their apparent disinclination to do so.

Douglas Adams

British Rail's anti-snow measures did not work because the wrong kind of snow fell.

Terry Worrall

The shortest distance between two points is always under construction.

Noelie Altito

Even Napoleon had his Watergate.

Yogi Berra

I have an existential map. It has 'You are here' written all over it.

Steven Wright

As I was being helped over the rail of the *Titanic* I said, 'I rang for ice, but this is ridiculous'.

Madeline Astor

Only brave mouse makes nest in cat's ear.

Charlie Chan

I could have become a soldier if I had waited; I knew more about retreating than the man who invented retreating.

Mark Twain

Whatever is not nailed down is mine. Whatever I can pry loose is not nailed down.

Collis Huntington

I asked the landlady what her weekly rates were and she said that nobody had ever stayed a week.

Frank Carson

You have won a week's free holiday in Vietnam at our new hotel. It's five star and you can see three of them through the roof.

Mike Swan

My girlfriend told me to take a heavy sweater to Edinburgh so I brought Luther Vandross.

Steve Jay

Differently clued.

Dave Clark

See a pin and pick it up – all day long you'll have a pin.

Audrey Austin

I'm not a complete idiot. Some of the parts are missing.

Emo Philips

I used your soap two years ago; since then I have used no other.

Mister Punch

Miscellaneous

At three in the morning, the hotel foyer has the desperate air of the last ladies-excuse-me on the *Titanic*.

A.A. Gill

What colour does a smurf turn when you choke it?

Steven Wright

You can save money on expensive personalised car plates by simply changing your name to match your existing plate.

KVL 741

I have a full size map of the world but I hardly ever unroll it.

Steven Wright

Today I saw a subliminal advertising executive for just a second.

Steven Wright

Who buys coat hangers? They breed in your closet like rattlesnakes.

Stuart McLean

I'm reading the dictionary backwards looking for subliminal messages.

Steven Wright

He had double chins all the way down to his stomach.

Mark Twain

Douglas Haig was brilliant to the top of his army boots.

David Lloyd-George

Ah, what is man? Wherefore does he why? Whence did he whence? Whither is he whithering?

Dan Leno

I couldn't repair my brakes, so I made my horn louder.

Steven Wright

If it ain't broke, break it.

Bob Judge

One morning I shot an elephant in my pajamas. How he got into my pajamas I'll never know.

Groucho Marx

Invite all encylopaedia salesmen in. Nip out the back door. Phone the police and tell them your house is being burgled.

Mike Harding

It was so cold that the local flashers were handing out written descriptions.

Roy Brown

Vital papers will demonstrate their vitality by spontaneously moving from where you left them to where you can't find them.

Robert Murphy

The beautiful woman at the bar said to me 'You're wearing two different coloured socks', and I said 'I know, but to me they're the same, I go by thickness'.

Steven Wright

The direct use of force is such a poor solution to any problem that it is generally employed only by small children and large nations.

David Friedman

My wife was unable to obtain a hotel room with a bidet. I suggested that she do a handstand in the shower.

Billy Wilder

Accomplishing the impossible means only that the boss will add it to your regular duties.

Doug Larson

He doesn't know much but he leads the league in nostril hair.

Josh Billings

When everything is coming your way, you're in the wrong traffic lane.

Steven Wright

He may look like an idiot and talk like an idiot but don't let that fool you. He really is an idiot.

Groucho Marx

If we don't change direction soon, we'll end up where we're going.

Irwin Corey

If forced to travel on an airplane, try to get in the cabin with the Captain, so you can keep an eye on him and nudge him if he falls asleep or point out any mountains looming up ahead.

Mike Harding

If a subordinate asks you a pertinent question, look down at him as if he had lost his senses. When he looks down, paraphrase the question back at him.

Samuel Spark

Mahaffy was caned only once in his life, and that was for telling the truth – but it certainly cured him.

George Salmon

I treasure every moment that I do not see Phyllis Diller.

Oscar Levant

Once you could open postal packets with your bare hands. Who would think of tackling one today with anything less than a power-saw?

Kingsley Amis

Index

Index

Index

 **Index**

Index

Index

Index

Index

Index

Index

Index

Index

Index

Index

+ Receipt

+ Whiskey improves
   with age

* 2 years ago I gave
up drinking & sex
(worst 20 minutes of
   my life

Lager food. Scotch
         on rocks